The Human Face
of Negotiation

A tool to defuse anger, and other persuasions strategies

Julio Decaro

Medical Doctor, Universidad de la República, Uruguay
Executive Director of CMI Interser, Cambridge, USA.

© 2017 ALL RIGHTS RESERVED
Julio Decaro - CMI interser
Montevideo - Uruguay

Graphic Design: Pablo Decaro
Cover design: Pablo Decaro
Edition: February 2017

CONTENTS

Acknowledgments

I thank each and every person I ran into in this life, starting by my parents for who I am, what I say and do, even this book is a result of experiences lived when interacting with them.

Yet, specifically regarding this book, I am uniquely thankful to some.

To Lilian, for her ceaseless patience and for always providing her wise advice, courage and support.

To Professor Robert Kertesz for his unforgettable teachings, his intelligent and creative view of things, his exceptional innovative talent and integrative skills, and, above all, for his generosity in his constant support towards Lilian and me.

To Professor Dr. Roger Fisher, for his inspirational work, what I have learned from him and the model he created are the foundations of my book.

To Dr. Danny Ertel, for his friendship, for supporting me in my first developments and in writing my first articles on the topic, for trusting me and giving me the opportunity to get involved in this passionate world I work in.

To my partners, Mark Smith and Francisco Sanchez for our bonding brotherhood, their unconditional support and for contributing their model of life, exemplary of what we preach.

To Horacio Falcao, for the energy and passion he places on all things and which encouraged the publication of this book.

To Ana Fierro, my secretary, for her enriching and clarifying arrangements and excellent diagrams, and also to Maria Eugenia Ferolla, for her patience and invaluable support in my daily work beyond this book.

Dedication

Some time ago I was in Montevideo and I received an e-mail from a friend with a story my partner Francisco Sanchez had told at Cambridge one month before. When I heard the story told again, this time from a priest in a sermon delivered in Washington, I thought I had to make it known even if I was not familiar with the author.

"Once a professor showed his students a large jar, similar to a fishbowl, and asked, Is it full or empty?

They all answered it was empty.

Very well, replied the professor, and took out several large stones from a bag and poured them into the fishbowl until it was full.

He then asked once more if the jar was full.

The students responded with a unanimous "yes".

Out of another bag, he took out small pebbles and poured them in. These started rolling between the larger ones filling the spaces.

He then asked the students if the jar was full.

The majority hesitated, some answered it was full and others said it was partly empty.

The Professor then produced sand out of another bag, and poured it into the small spaces still remaining in between the pebbles until there was room for no more. He asked again: How is the jar now?

They all smiled. Some paused to answer and the majority said the jar was still not full.

The Professor then took a jug of water and poured it into the jar effectively filling the space between the grains of sand. Now, he asked: What is the meaning, the teachings of what you have just seen?

Rumors, shifts, thoughtful faces ensued until one student raised his hand and said: The take home message is that no matter how busy we are, how overburdened with work or how involved, there will always be room for something more.

No, answered the professor emphatically — the lesson is, the rocks go first."

To Lilian, the underpinnings of my life and my greatest project: my family.

Introduction

"Excellence comes from devoting yourself passionately to a single
perspective.

Genius comes from passionate devotion to integrating
several perspectives.

Wisdom comes from a passionate devotion to
relate several perspectives."

Robert Dilts

In this book you will not find a new theory on negotiation since, as members
of CMIIG, we strongly believe in Roger Fisher's principled negotiation (*Harvard
University Negotiation Project Method*) which you will notice in frequent references
and connections of it throughout the chapters. In addition, we also use some of
our customary working tools.

It therefore adds to the philosophical win-win approach or culture in
negotiations and conflict resolution though from a different perspective. This
approach defines "winning" or "being successful" in a negotiation as one where
the result attained:

- Satisfied interests: mine, theirs too (or at least acceptably) and third
  parties' tolerably. It was an efficient solution, with no waste: the best
  option among many created.
- It was legitimate to all, nobody felt cheated.
  It was better than my best alternative (better than what I could have
  obtained alone or with another.)
- Was shaped into a realistic, operational and functional commitment. In
  addition, the process was efficient.
- There was good communication.
- I strengthened my desired relationship.

For all of the above, and since this is not a book on how to take advantage of the other side in a negotiation setting, if you wish to improve the way in which you negotiate or solve your differences, once you are done reading, my best recommendation is: Instead of holding on to the knowledge acquired or putting the book away on a bookshelf, loan it to someone with whom you will negotiate. I can assure you you will obtain better outcomes. If, however, you wish to enlarge on some of the notions of the Harvard Negotiation Project Theory, I recommend reading *Getting to Yes. Negotiating Agreement Without Giving In*, by R. Fisher, W. Ury and B. Patton., a detailed description of the core of the method.

All negotiations carry two key elements that determine success: the type of communication and the working relationship negotiators are able to create or establish.

Good communication is the foundation of any proactive system, and it means:

Being effective, that is where the parties to the negotiation achieve clear and concise understanding of the messages, focusing on the principle of functionality and quality of information conveyed;

Being efficient, that is, it does not take a lifetime to achieve such understanding;

Instead of communicating **to** the other party, negotiators communicate **with** them. And, rather than presenting their arguments, they are also able to actively listen and ask for the purpose of understanding and learning, like a two-way road, using feedback, where each party ensures understanding and having been understood.

Both parties should be able to present their points of view and conclusions, but also explain to others where the data came from and the underlying and underpinnings of their rationale and interpretations.

A good working relationship means treating those you will be negotiating with cordially and respectfully.

A good working relationship means, among other things:

• Knowing how to assertively resolve differences, i.e. neither submissively nor aggressively.

• Knowing how to separate the people from the problem; being mutually respectful, understanding, and accepting of each other as human beings, even when dealing firmly with the substance.

- Being able to handle and balance feelings and logic.
- Knowing how to build a mutually credible and trusting setting.

Developing your personal skills in these two areas will guarantee better negotiation results, especially if you decide to do so proactively, that is, leading the initiative and taking on responsibility for the outcomes. You must unreservedly keep a constructive mindset, whether there is reciprocity or not.

Yet, I will not say that it is better to communicate well than do it badly, and that you must achieve a good working relationship with your negotiating counterpart; *that* you already know. What I will do is share some strategies, techniques and tools taken from psychotherapy and negotiation fields on how to achieve those goals.

This is a book that deals with relationships, a true negotiation between the world of psychology and the world of negotiation per se.

Its technical and scientific contributions are the result of integrating the *Harvard Negotiation Project* perspective and some psychological concepts I consider interesting on new behavioral sciences, applicable and adaptable to this context. Readers who know about psychology may be able to recognize ideas and tools I have borrowed, adapted and integrated from different disciplines in that field (short therapies, Eriksonian hypnosis, gestalt, etc.), but primarily from *Transactional Analysis* (Eric Berne) and *Neurolinguistic Programming* (NLP) (Richard Randler and John Grinder). I thank all my mentors in these arts and their creators, especially, Doctor Robert Kertesz, who got me started in these disciplines.

This book is about a set of essays whose common denominator is the search for greater understanding of the impact of the human dimension in negotiations, and how to tap into such understanding in order to improve results for all parties involved.

For two main aspects: On the one hand, the universal nature of relationships and communication issues in negotiation and life in general, and, on the other, the strategic and non-tactical level of approaches, ideas, suggestions, techniques and tools of different writings will be useful and applicable to your own life moments and situations.

The notions contained in this book are applicable to any negotiation you might be involved in during your life, be it conflicts, domestic negotiations (family, couple or daily interpersonal ones) or more complex scenarios, whether commercial and work-related (organizational, interinstitutional, international), social or political.

Generically speaking, best results are obtained in negotiations where a long term relationship is important, that is, those negotiations that continue over time, involving —though we may not be aware of it— more than two parties and mutliple issues: some are tangible, like money, goods or services; some intangible, like trust, reputation or precedent. These are definitely how the majority of our negotiations look like, those with our spouses, children, neighbors, bosses, collaborators, clients and customers, suppliers, and friends, etc.

Whatever the situation, this book will help you solve problems that have always been considered hard to manage in negotiations, such as:

- Time management in negotiations; and avoid falling into psychological games.

- Asking good questions.

- Classifying people. Acting in the face of risk. Generating trust and credibility.

- Managing anger and aggression.

- Shielding yourself from being taken advantage of or from those who try to manipulate, blackmail or make you feel guilty or afraid.

- Knowledge of yourself and others to exercise persuasion.

In summary, this book is the result of pursuing conceptual and practical answers to some of the most difficult questions found in trainings and consulting work.

It is essentially a practical book. In each writing piece you will find a brief theoretical framework as supporting material to conceptually understand the topic, as well as examples and short stories which will not only make the reading more pleasant but also help illustrate ideas and tools for daily use.

It is impossible to attribute an intrinsically moral value to the majority of tools presented in different chapters, as would be the case if we attributed value to the act of persuading or influencing others. As Professor Fisher says, "In a situation of conflict the morality of an action is frequently measured not by assessing the nature itself of the action, but by measuring its consequences", and later on states in his book *Beyond Machiavelli*: "In short, if moral positions are adopted based on possible consequences to suggested decisions, a moral requirement is added to the existing pragmatism: calculating possible results of one's own actions, and assessing the good and bad in them."

Fisher proposes in a simpler way to ask yourself a set of questions that force you -when honestly answered- to think about certain ethical criteria before making a proposal (using a technique or tool), e.g.: If I were to analyze a certain behavior years from now, or if I appeared in the headlines of some newspaper tomorrow,

Is it more likely that I'll be proud or feel shame and be sorry about it?

Will I be acknowledged for it or will I have to defend myself?

Would I be pleased if it were used for a family member?

Would I want my children to use it as a guideline for future actions?

Is it legal? Is it consistent with the creation and prudent interpretation of fair laws?

Is it consistent with different religious teachings around the world?

How would a novelist describe my behavior? Closer to that of a hero or villain?

A basic idea that can help guide our own behavior regarding the use of knowledge, a strategy, technique or tool in a given situation is "[...] seek to minimize the things we might have to repent of later and maximize the chances to continue thinking (rationally or gut feeling) that we did what was the most fair."

This in no way means that two people considered equally ethical will reach the same verdict, but "if we know the goals were carefully defined, the means to attain them were rigorously designed and that both ends and means were consciously assessed in the light of high values, that is all you can ask for."

Finally, the guidelines and recommendations will show you with ease how to apply the different tools. Given that each essay is a unit in and of itself, each could be read separately and in no fixed order, though I suggest reading them in the order they appear.

Enjoy the reading!

CHAPTER 1

Do Opposites Attract?

Magnets Do, Humans Don't.

1

> You are a very smart person because you think just like me!
>
> Alvaro Mas

Creating a Good Working Relationship Is a Task

Experience shows that negotiations that attain the best results are those where participants focus on exploring the interests of the parties involved, developing creative options and supporting these with objective legitimacy criteria, separate from the will of the negotiators.

However, it is not always possible to deal with these topics that aim towards the core of the negotiation until a good working relationship is established. This does not necessarily mean becoming friends with the other party or inviting them over for dinner; rather to help negotiation participants be able to overcome their differences in a civilized and assertive way, and, especially, create a reliable and credible setting to enable parties to reach better results, not just short term but also mid and long term results.

Nevertheless, people involved in preparing for a negotiation are often surprised when asked about the type of relationship they wish to establish and what they think of doing to achieve it.

Most of the times, this element —without which the others would be senseless— is not considered because it is believed it happens naturally.

Some people think that a good working relationship is something spontaneous. However, leaving such an important and volatile element up to spontaneity may be risky at the time of negotiating, or at least it may mean losing good opportunities of establishing the groundwork of the remaining elements in negotiation.

A suitable working relationship is like oil to an engine: its existence facilitates the development of negotiations and the lack of it may lead to a halt. Encouraging a good working relationship is the main goal of negotiations and requires preparation, technique and skill. Like in many other things in life, you need to have a clear objective and a relevant strategy. In doing so, it is advisable to ask yourself a set of questions:

- What type of relationship am I in today with the person I will be negotiating with?
- What type of relationship do I want in the future?

  If the answers to these questions are different, the next questions are:

- What is causing such differences?
- What will I do to achieve my goal? What will my strategy be? Which are some specific actions to take?
- What evidence will I use to show I am achieving it?
- What other things can I do if I'm unsuccessful or if something unexpected prevents me from attaining it?

In Building a Good Relationship, Better Be Gracious Than Facetious

One of the most universal and most applicable principles in the field of human relationships in general, and, of course, in negotiations could be expressed thus: When we like someone it is less likely that we will want to disagree with that person, and we will most likely respond positively to his or her requests.

The implications of this generalization are very important for any type of relationship, but even more so in negotiations, where results depend on the ability to persuade and achieve affirmative answers to requests or respective proposals.

If this statement is true, the next rational question will be: How do we define the people we like?

The specific questions to ask are:

- How are the people with whom I get along better like?
- What makes that happen?
- What must a person say, do, think or feel for me to like him or her or to create a good communication with me?

People Like Us

During the years I worked as marketing director of a direct sales enterprise (similar to the Avon sales system), one of the first criteria for selecting salespeople —called beauty consultants—, was to be homemakers and neighbors, since the target market were neighboring women.

This apparently simple selection criterion had a very powerful rationale to it, and is as follows: one of the most compelling reasons why we like some people is because they are akin to us.

It is understood that when we say «people like us» or «similar to us» it does not mean they are identical. It refers to the fact that in some respects their world and ours have something in common. The more the points of agreement, the more you may relate.

How Are We Similar?

Sometimes, like in the statement by Dr. Mas at the beginning of this chapter, the point of agreement might be shared opinions on something (a problem, politics, football or any other subject.)

At others, what is shared may relate to relevant aspects such as race, religion, nationality, some personality traits, a political party, lifestyle, profession or interests, values and beliefs regarding various aspects of life.

In some instances, and according to context, other less relevant aspects create the same effect such as sharing a pastime, having a common acquaintance or friend, having visited same places, or even trivial details like sharing the same car model or sports club.

Other less apparent or less conscious elements, yet not necessarily less compelling, are also able to create that similarity or likeness: clothing, the way of speaking (volume, tone, pitch, speed, accent, etc.), the way of walking, posture, facial gestures or body movement.

Since typically the world and others are judged by our own parameters and points of view, similarity is that silent, unaware criterion with which each individual selects the majority of the people he or she relates to in his or her life: friends, collaborators and partner.

Being neighbors, that is, living in the same neighborhood, entails a combination of many of the similarities mentioned earlier, though not always: socioeconomic or cultural level, sometimes race or nationality, etc. This is the reason why it was the first criterion for selecting beauty consultants in the door-to-door sales system illustrated earlier.

The myth heading this chapter that "opposites attract" may be somewhat true or there may be exceptions confirming that rule. Many people could say they have friends that are different from them. In some cases those differences add spice to a relationship based on similarities. However, it is quite difficult to imagine a good relationship based on differences, discrepancies and conflict.

Now fully expressed, the principle states: If we are alike, you will like me, and if you like me, it is less likely that you will want to disagree with me and more likely that you will respond positively to my requests.

Equalizers or Differentiators

People could be classified into those who perceive and predominantly emphasize differences between ideas, situations or people, called differentiators, and those who more easily perceive similarities, what is alike between situations or people, those called equalizers.

Operating in one of these modes is not generically good, bad or worse than any other, yet there are situations, moments or even sequences where it is more efficient to apply one or another way of processing matters.

For example, during the process of creating options and presenting new ideas to resolve a problem in a negotiation, it is best to have equalizers analyze those ideas first. They will most likely find a way for that new idea to work and then let the differentiators do so. The latter will probably find a counter example, a situation or circumstances where that idea will fail. The opposite sequence, i.e. criticize new ideas first, is not the most appropriate or recommended one when pursuing creative ways of problem solving.

The task of building a good relationship, communicating, synchronizing or generating likeness to another or others benefits from emphasizing similarities, therefore making use of all equalizer skills available.

In conflicting situations, in negotiations and in everyday life, when the goal is to reach the solution to a problem, it is not advisable to start off focusing on disagreements, that which sets apart, or separates parties.

As a rule of thumb, transforming a minor agreement into a major one is infinitely easier than transforming a disagreement into an agreement.

An Unparalleled Equalizer

One of this century's most famous character in the field of medicine, and especially in psychiatry, is Dr. Milton Erickson, the father of modern hypnosis. Few persons have been so keenly studied and analyzed as Dr. Erickson to discover the secret of his intervention strategies and skill at influencing and persuading especially difficult people.

After a long period of direct observation and examination of film shootings made by his students and expert analysts, it was discovered, among other things, that not many individuals could equal Dr. Erickson's' ability to so quickly generate a superb communication and working relationship with his clients. For Erickson there were no refractory patients, only therapists with scarce flexibility.

Rapport, conformity, agreement, alignment, likeness, familiarity, similarity, affinity, harmony, acceptance, wellbeing and belonging are some of the nouns used to describe the results of a technique known as pacing, one of the greatest secrets of success.

Pacing (to go to the beat of) precisely means to seek the place where our world and the other person's world meet; a point of agreement, a place where the beginning of similarity is applicable to a given situation.

Finding the other person at his or her own level entails matching or equating some aspect of their behavior, thoughts or emotions. It comprises presenting or highlighting to those you are negotiating or living with, your own aspects that are the closest or most similar to theirs.

Pacing means creating a connection of respect, understanding and acceptance of the other's point of view, which does not necessarily imply agreement.

Pacing is communication, perhaps the most basic and compelling way of communicating. When pacing is used you are somehow telling the other party to rest assured that there are similarities. Here, one of the subtlest forms is being applied to generate credibility and trust between people, two of the most important values for establishing a good working relationship needed for achieving successful negotiations.

Gorilas in the Mist, the film based on the life and work of the famous anthropologist Dian Fossey, is one of the most illustrative examples of the power of this technique. In this case it exceeds the limits of communication between humans to show its effectiveness; even between men and primates.

Pacing is Natural

Pacing is something for which human beings are well prepared; something that is learned from our parents ever since birth and that occurs naturally all the time.

Recalling the bodily posture, gestures and the way of speaking adopted by adults when they wish to generate good communication with a small child illustrates the concept, and how simple and spontaneous it is for the majority of people to physically pace with others.

If you think of how hard it is not to yawn when others do, or not to replicate the stuttering or tics of someone you are talking with, or not feel the lack of air when in presence of someone during an asthma attack; all these help understand the natural human trend to pace.

If you listen and watch carefully at restaurants, offices and public places where people meet, talk and stride, you will notice with what ease and how natural it is for those who are in synch to pace and harmonize. Even more so, it is easy to see who are *not* pacing, although you may not know what they are talking about.

If a Latino travels to some other Spanish speaking country and lives there for a while, his or her accent will change and adapt to that of the place, to such an extent that it may sometimes be absolutely no different from a local. The popular saying "when in Rome do as the Romans" is an abridged version of the same principle. Conventional wisdom says that when you visit a foreign place you must use pacing, it is a way of feeling alike and allowing for better adjustment.

In order to live together in society you must pace each moment with the people and general situations, like the dress code, or the silence you keep when entering a temple, regardless of your religious beliefs.

However, the natural predisposition to pace may be improved (like in so many other skills) if consciously paid attention to and practiced. That is the goal of this chapter.

What To Pace

The entire world or any situation in life, including of course our daily negotiations, may be a reason to find similarities that unite or differences that divide.

If the purpose is to pace, there are endless levels and situations, from the most trivial to the most significant, the most obvious to those less conscious where you can find or create a point of agreement between your own world and that of other negotiators.

♦ Values, beliefs, interests and opinions about things

Sometimes you can be in synch with a person's values and beliefs; understand and share what that person thinks is the truth, or is worth it or of interest, according to his or her own way of seeing t absolute terms, this is not the most common situation in conflict Though, in negotiation settings. Nevertheless, even in the light of deep antagonism it is possible to find some shared supra-value.

For example, in the political arena it is frequently observed that two steadfast adversaries with deep differences occasionally do reach negotiated agreements based on their convergence on the importance, mutual value and interest in preserving democracy or national wellbeing above any partisan color.

Often negotiations become stagnated on account of positions which, when carefully explored, reveal some shared and complementary interests underlying antagonistic positions.

Carefully exploring interests that underlie parties' positions and underscoring similarities or different yet complementary interests is a good pacing strategy and more appropriate than to start off by dealing with clearly opposite and conflicting interests.

Other times, to start negotiating and reaching agreement on the negotiation process, i.e. how to negotiate and establishing some basic rules, may, in difficult situations, be a good way of pacing; a chance to create a common point of interest, an understanding that does not jeopardize the substance of the negotiation which is often burdened with more complex subjects.

At least, what you can always do to pace some specific belief, value or interest is to understand and validate the other person's right to a different point of view on some fact or circumstance, although not in agreement. Acknowledging this right and understanding — though not sharing the idea— may often be enough to find a point of agreement and appropriately start the relationship needed.

In fact, persuasion relates to validating the other party's perspective as one among many possible ones, and later considering, and, in time, accepting other options. Accepting the other person's perspective often leads to that party's acceptance of our point of view, though not always.

In this field, it is important to be able to distinguish between a principle: that of paramount importance for which even your life could be at stake, and what is a debatable issue: that for which you may only have an opinion.

The ideal situation in negotiations is being firm on principles and flexible on opinions, and have the ability to set them apart. Flexibility is the key skill. In any human, mechanical or electronic system, including of course negotiating systems, if all other things remain equal, the prevailing element will be the one that has the widest range of possible answers.

Finally, all negotiations have some rituals, preliminaries or pastimes. If flexibility is considered as a value, you will always be able to find some conversation topics of interest to the other party that may be useful to create similarities without involving great risk.

◆ Body Language

Whether there is agreement or not regarding the sweeping statement that 93% of the weight of communication is attributed to the process, body language and the communication mode, and only 7% to word content and the substance of communication, we must acknowledge that body language is compelling and has such weight that it becomes transcendental when establishing a relationship in the negotiation field or any other circumstance in life.

In negotiation, when gestures do not match what is being said, the best case scenario will find the counterparty confused; yet most of the time, the opposite party will believe in what he or she sees. Being alert to your own and your counterparty's body language is the first step to a possible pacing strategy at a level that is not quite conscious to the majority, and, therefore, very powerful.

As mentioned earlier, observing people while seated at restaurants or talking at work meetings and negotiations where you cannot hear what they are saying, is an excellent place to discover, either by the similarity or disparity of postures, gestures and movements, who is in synch or in agreement and who is not.

Sharing some behavioral patterns: type, rhythm and range of movements; some gestures; body postures; distance, and even clothing help create a feeling of correspondence, acceptance, belonging and wellbeing known as interactional synchrony. If attention is closely paid, it is easily perceived in the young, in businesses, social meetings or in any setting. This synchrony sends a message to the other party, silently and out of conscious control, saying that they are alike.

When this occurs naturally, the components of body language take place at different times during conversations, in a sequence that recalls the rhythm of a dance.

This also includes handling physical spaces. For example, sitting face to face or side by side makes a difference in negotiation meetings. Sitting side by side to the person you are negotiating with, i.e. aligning your body so that both point in the same direction, maybe facing a flipchart or a sheet of paper on the table where you are writing down the problem, implies an act of communication: there is a common problem to solve, there are two people, and they are both seeing it from the same position or perspective.

♦ The process of verbal language

Pacing another person's verbal communication has two possible components: one is related to the volume, speed, pitch, rhythm and tone of speech; the other is words, sentences and the type of metaphors used to represent reality.

Trying to equate (pace) as far as possible both components during a conversation creates in the listener a familiar, unconscious feeling of something true, intelligent or real.

Using a similar tone and volume of voice; comparable speed; using words that are significant to the other person, i.e. words frequently used by that person; emphasizing what is being said and explaining own concepts through phrases and metaphors belonging to the context and daily life of the other party, or related to topics that are familiar, encourage the feeling that both speak the same language, and, therefore, are alike.

Occasionally, when people do not speak the same language, knowing and using at least a few words of the other's language is enough to create rapport.

Every time Professor Roger Fisher starts a talk for a Spanish-speaking audience, he says: "*Buenos días*" (in Spanish) and after he goes on to say, in English: "Now you know everything I know in Spanish." The audience laughs and Roger earns the sympathy of the attendants.

Whereas, using unintelligible jargon towards the other party, often times typical of a certain commercial sector, profession or culture, means underscoring differences and creating distance. Somebody that speaks slowly and deliberately will be thankful if the speaker does not shout or overwhelm him or her by the speed of his or her words.

Speaking at a speed or tone of voice or volume that is totally different from that of the other side may create a barrier and feeling of disagreement, even when the content does not show substantial differences.

Verbally pacing may deeply influence a relationship that is being created with another person. Handling this technique becomes much more important when negotiating over the phone where the voice is the only resource available for persuasion.

♦ The content of verbal language

In negotiation, the content of what is being said may be one of the hardest parts to pace since parties may not always agree with the content expressed. However, it is possible to use verbal language content for pacing, even if there is disagreement with the other party. By repeating word for word what the other party has just said, together with a tone of voice showing sincere curiosity, at least points out understanding of what was said though eventually not sharing those ideas.

If one party says to the other: "Let me see if I understood what you have just said," and immediately proceeds to repeat it, this instantly creates a positive answer: "Yes, that is what I meant", and, therefore, reaching a minimum point of agreement.

Paraphrasing, i.e. rephrasing what the other party has said slightly changing the phrase construction has the same effect, and is even subtler, if it is accompanied by a similar tone of curiosity.

Paraphrasing and enlarging, that is, adding your own opinion or idea to the paraphrase, though slightly riskier creates similar results.

Repeating any of these techniques or combination thereof during conversations —provided there is no overuse— helps create some pacing moments in negotiations, all of which preserve the relationship, even in situations of significant divergence on the substance.

♦ Breathing

Pacing the breathing rhythm of another person is one of the subtlest, most unconscious, powerful and oldest ways ever recorded. It is greatly applied in the field of hypnosis and psychotherapy. In the business environment it is generally inappropriate, and, obviously, in multiparty negotiations it is absolutely impossible.

♦ Moods and Emotions

> Occasionally, people we interact with in negotiations may present different moods at different moments during the process. Generally speaking, it is not convenient to pace some of these moods, as is the case with anger. Although sometimes raising your voice deliberately and showing limits leads to some beneficial results, as a general rule it is not convenient to escalate verbal aggression, and even less so get involved in emotions. The reader should refer to the chapter on the *Loser Strategy* for a more elegant and efficient suggestion to handle these situations.

> Nevertheless, for other moods, like depression or worry, pacing may be the first recommended step for changing them. Replicating what the other person feels through gestures, voice tone and volume, and occasionally through verbal understanding and rapport enables access to a more productive mood, faster than if attempts are made to demean others for their feelings. Few things can cause such negative effect as telling someone who is depressed or worried that there is no reason for such mood yet said in an overjoyed tone. Not only does this put down the person's emotions but also makes the person feel he or she cannot handle feelings well.

What Not to Pace

Although sometimes hard to handle, it is recommended not to pace nervous tics, mannerisms, foreign accents, stutters or any other type of behavior that, when matched, might be wrongly interpreted by the other person.

Neither is it recommended to pace beliefs or values contrary to a person's basic principles; or aggressive behavior.

Pacing followed by leading means to seek or create likeness as the first step of a strategy that later shows what is different. One of the most effective persuasion strategies since the beginning of time is finding a point of agreement that helps create credibility and trust to later move towards what is different. It is infinitely better than trying to persuade starting off by differences.

Let us recall the general rule: It is infinitely easier to move from a minor agreement to a major agreement than from disagreement to agreement.

The one who paces others first has more chances of being followed. In negotiation, raising differences first tends to create resistance and make matters worse when trying to change the system.

When Is It Time to Start Leading?

The time during which it is necessary to pace to later start leading varies from negotiation to negotiation. In some situations, the period of pacing may be short; in others it is best not to attempt leading too soon.

It is a matter of trial and error. If during the attempt to lead you find resistance from the other negotiator, it is recommended to resume pacing and wait for a new opportunity to attempt leading later on. Remember, if something does not work it is advisable to stop and do something else.

In most negotiations the game of pacing, leading and pacing again to once again start leading should be repeated many times, as many as necessary.

Value Added

In preparation for the settlement process, various negotiation schools recommend putting yourself in the other person's shoes. It is very beneficial to understand how the other side thinks and feels and what are some of their interests and options to reach a workable agreement, from their perspective. Establishing some of these elements often enables foreseeing and anticipating possible answers and behaviors from others when faced with various proposals.

Putting yourself in someone else's shoes may take place rationalizing (alone or with others) a systematic preparation toolkit. It can also be achieved through simulation by roleplaying the relevant person.

Nevertheless, during the negotiation pacing has an impact not only on one of the parties; the impact is on both. Adopting different positions serves the purpose, like in the theatre, for the appearance of different characters on stage. The way of speaking, thinking and feeling is different according to the physical position adopted. Attitudes change if a person is lying down, sitting up or feeling uncomfortable.

Experiencing rapport with another person, adopting that person's posture, gestures and way of speaking is like being in that person's body or mind. This provides new and distinct information; it opens the road to a deeper understanding of the person's thoughts, emotions and perspectives. With practice you can at times be able to think and feel like the other party which enables leading more appropriately and respectfully. However, this also carries some risks.

It is possible that when pacing and putting yourself in someone else's shoes, you may develop such empathy that occasionally you will think the other side is right or conclude that your own arguments are really weak to achieve the desired change.

In any case, you must decide what to do with the additional information that accounts for an added value to the negotiator who possesses it.

Two Complementary Skills

After setting the goal, whatever the negotiation outlook or situation you decided to pace as part of the strategy for creating a good working relationship, you must develop perceptual acuity as a complementary skill.

Since the communication message boils down to the receiver's answer, being alert, sharpening all senses and capturing reactions on others are prerequisites to determine, for example, the appropriate element for pacing, the right time to lead, the convenience of resuming pacing and the relevance of doing something different.

Considering this last point, the second complementary skill is flexibility, because if what is done to pace and lead proves unsuccessful, a different strategy should be promoted.

Some General Recommendations for Practice

Like any human ability, the capacity to create alignment and synchrony improves with practice, but the following is recommended:

- ♦ Do not miss any opportunity to practice. Doing so does not require being engaged in a formal negotiation. Practice every day. If you do not want to run any risk, at first you can practice in front of the television set or walking on the street. In doing so you can follow from a few steps behind someone who walks really differently from you and pace the person with that stride: no one will probably notice it but in this exercise you can physically perceive the discomfort of the difference, and shortly after a new world of sensations, thoughts and emotions ensues.

- ♦ Test one element at a time: at the beginning it is not advisable to try mixing many techniques.

- ♦ Choose the element you intuitively consider easier to pace. It is often simpler to start pacing the way the other person speaks (tone, rhythm, volume.)

- ♦ As you become familiar with different elements you will be able to use the one that proves easier or more convenient according to the situation. For example, if a negotiator does not look at the speaker when talking or keeps a low gaze, verbal pacing is the most appropriate.

- ♦ Lastly, it is not hard to use several types of pacing simultaneously, and though the attention at first may detour from the conversation content, there is no need to worry: all people repeat the same idea during a conversation, speech or writing, as you would be able to prove if you were to review this chapter.

Therefore: Is Pacing Negotiation's Magic Pill?

Decidedly not.

Creating good rapport is a prerequisite to effective communication and for other negotiation elements to operate under better conditions.

Pacing can generate goodwill from the other side yet developing a lasting relationship and satisfactory results in negotiations requires more than that.

It cannot replace competence. Creating a favorable environment is a complement and not a substitute for the skill or competence to:

♦ Listen to and establish a good two-way communication.

♦ Discover interests behind positions and be able to satisfy them.

♦ Generate creative options, with value added elements for all parties.

♦ Be supportive of arguments with legitimacy criteria and let yourself be persuaded by others' legitimate reasons.

♦ Establish intelligent, realistic, operational and functional commitments.

♦ Develop a good alternative in case agreement is not reached.

It does not replace good faith or the philosophy of respect and mutual gain. If the goal is to employ this tool to later manipulate and use people; in addition to making the other side feel temporarily well, if you are not able to think long term, consider their interests and needs honestly, candidly and respectfully, you may be able to accomplish something at first but soon enough results will reveal the short term effect of your ploy.

Do Opposites Attract?

Creating a good long term working relationship implies good pacing skills and also requires:

Accepting the other side as a person and knowing he or she may have a different view, though not shared.

Establishing a good two-way communication.

Understanding each other even when there is disagreement.

Balancing emotions and reason.

Being unconditionally reliable.

Using persuasion rather than manipulation.

CHAPTER 2
When and How Separating
People is Useful

A Practical Guide to Classify the World

> First classification of the world: The world is classified into those who use umbrella
> and those who don't.
> Second classification of the world: The world is classified into those who classify the world
> into those who use umbrella and those who don't, and those who don't classify the world.
> Unknown author.

Human Beings Are Creatures of Habit

Is it possible to know someone so much that you are able to assert with high chances of getting it right that, faced with a given fact or situation, such person will act as usual and therefore predictably?

Probably so. This is likely to occur with people you have been living longer with, whether relatives, fellow workers, clients, friends or neighbors. In summary, people with whom you constantly negotiate.

Time and observation (even the unconscious type) enable us to recognize certain patterns of behavior, response or preference for certain people which under specific conditions allow some facts to be predicted.

Predictable behavior in humans answers to programs created at some point in their lives; they depend on some generalizations made, shortcuts each person's biocomputer has developed for surviving in a complex world.

The Origin of Our Habits

In some cases, it is pretty simple to point out to the situation or events in people's lives that led to some routine behavioral patterns or even to some of their more salient skills, capacities or values and beliefs.

In this regard, it is interesting to examine the perspective presented by Garcia and Dolan in their book *Managing by Values*, where they state: "Values are learnings relatively stable over time where one way of acting is better than its opposite in order for things to work out well."

Sometimes, a single important and significant event, perhaps comprising a high degree of emotional involvement, is enough to achieve a learning experience, to shape a vision and determine how to perceive any future fact.

Other times they are low emotional impact situations but repeated over time during the most sensitive years in a human being's life (from birth till ages 6 and 8) which "culturalize" responses. In other cases, the events that gave rise to those programs are hidden to memory or awareness, and at times do not even belong to the person's own experience but rather to some previous 'programmer' or to the programmer's programmer.

Allow me to share a personal example to reinforce my words.

During lunch, dinner or any meal, I most likely will not leave leftovers on my plate, even if the amount is sizeable. I appreciate this can be detrimental to my health, but if I don't make a conscious effort to handle the situation my old program most certainly activates. In this case the programmer was my grandmother on my father's side, a chubby matron who would repeat in a very serious voice: "Better crash with food than throw in the trash", as she forced me to eat my apple to the core.

Such powerful mandate most likely stemmed from my grandmother's previous generation; Europeans who suffered all the calamities of war. In that context generalization takes on its real sense. However, in the absence of a voluntary wish to control it, this program would render my behavior absolutely predictable till this day, two generations later.

Microprograms, Macroprograms and Metaprograms

Although the example refers to a microprogram, during a lifetime the brain builds great generalizations that encompass more than one specific situation. These are called macroprograms and metaprograms, that is, programs from programs. Metaprograms become large thought filters that dictate preferential ways of perceiving reality, processing data internally, distinguishing points of agreement and establishing typical ways of responding to or undertaking behaviors.

Like all generalizations, these programs are our thoughts' shortcuts that help us live without having to think –whenever a decision-making situation arises– which of the many options to choose from hence simplifying procedures. Imagine how impossible life would be if every time you are standing in front of a door you had to think where the latch is and what side it swings open to. However, when a door swings open in the opposite direction, you can perceive the limitations of any generalization. The danger of great generalizations is precisely that it restrains options; sometimes to such an extent that answers seem to be automated responses thus reducing flexibility.

Many times we are not aware of what we do or how we do it, so the capacity to determine the convenience or functionality of our own programs is restricted.

When to Negotiate

Like in any other activity, when we negotiate our metaprograms as well as those of other negotiators' are triggered.

Since most complex personal negotiations repeat themselves over time with close people or acquaintants (bosses, collaborators, friends, clients, suppliers, spouses, children and neighbors), foresight is not only feasible but it becomes extremely important. Knowing yourself and knowing others is the foundation for anticipation.

When you are able to establish a process whereby a person makes certain types of decisions you are likely to increase your future decision-making foresight ability in similar situations.

Predicting and using some of the earlier mentioned aspects (values, beliefs, interests, preferential ways of information intake and processing, and behaviors in the light of certain situations) make a difference when negotiating.

Oftentimes, when issues are presented inappropriately, results of an excellent proposal may be ruined though perfectly convenient and viable in content. Being aware of your own metaprograms and those of your negotiating counterparts offers greater efficiency.

Noticing and using the other person's dominating ways of perceiving and processing information may imply additional efforts yet these will improve communication results, the working relationship, and therefore negotiations in the long run. In addition, the other party will be thankful, whether conscious or unconsciously, for your efforts in submitting ideas having considered their context and referents.

To Each His Own?

Yes, this is true; and metaprograms are specific to each person. Nevertheless, we can also generalize and cluster all those who show a similar style of processing information and knowledge into groups known nowadays in marketing as segments or audience.

How to classify (segment) people has been around for a very long time. Some of the most popular ones, for example the Zodiac signs, relate behaviors, strategies, motivations, and even personality and identity to the influential nature of the sign born under, and divide human beings into 12 groups, each governed by a sign.

Other ancient forms like the Enneagram, influenced by the search of God, establishes a relation with the capital sins and classifies people into nine types (Enneagram: *ennea = meaning nine; gramma = something "written" or "drawn"*.)

Hippocrates classified humans into four groups (sanguine, melancholic, choleric and phlegmatic) based on several body fluids (blood, black bile, yellow bile and phlegm) which were for a long time indicative not only of personality types but also predictors of certain physical illnesses.

Dozens of ways of classifying humans have been created ever since. Some of them are well known in the business world like the Myers-Briggs which, in turn, starts from a previous classification by Carl Jung, but all geared towards the same goal: anticipating behaviors, conduct, reactions, responses and even likely pathologies with the least possible error.

Within Effectiveness Seek the Most Practical

Considering that the above classifications are all ways of representing reality and not reality in and of itself, we can also state that some classifications are more practical and useful than others for certain purposes.

One of Professor Roger Fisher's stories is on the snake classification. He says that one of the most accurate ways of classifying them is by size (e.g. those that measure over one meter and those that measure less than a meter.) Another way of classifying snakes is: poisonous and non-poisonous snakes. The latter classification is not as accurate as the previous one since there are some mildly poisonous snakes, others moderately poisonous and some that are very poisonous, yet this classification is way more practical when confronted with an ophidian.

A Word of Caution

There follows a description of one type of classification and a brief summary of a few others.

The one I will enlarge on has the same virtues and limitations as the rest. It is only an effort to simplify the world in order to operate in a practical manner. In no way does it represent the whole truth, or reality or even the most accurate of all classifications (more than a meter or less than a meter), yet it is practical (poisonous or non-poisonous) and easy to apply when trying to attain results in negotiating with clients or managing interpersonal relationships in general.

The idea is to present an easy classification approach based on simple revealing elements for oneself and others. This approach should somehow offer guidelines or references on how to use predictions on the road to achieving goals in the negotiations we are involved in.

Classifying oneself or someone in one segment or another in any arrangement system does not imply being judgmental or expressing an opinion about what is right or wrong per se. At most you can reflect on whether a habit or pattern, be it your own or others', is the most appropriate in a given situation or context.

In this sense, flexibility is the most useful value, that is, the ability to use, based on a sound methodology, different ways of behaving when faced with distinct situations and people. Let us remember that: "In any system (machines or human), if all else remains equal, the individual (machine or human) with the widest range of response will control the system." (Law of requisite variety.)

Like many other things in life and unlike the astrological classification, many metaprograms referred to here are contextual. Lightly extrapolating forecasts made in a context (for example, work) onto others (for example family, fun time, and friends) can lead to mistakes. This does not rule out the fact that there are people with trans-contextual metaprograms, i.e. who show the same trends and ways of processing or responding regardless of the existing context.

What Is More Motivating: Power, Affiliation or Achievements?

Some people are basically motivated by aspects in life related to affiliation, i.e. what generically (though not exclusively) motives or interests them relates to:

- ♦ Participating in teams; working with people.

- ♦ Developing good interpersonal relations, pleasing, being accepted.

- ♦ Communicating warmly.

- ♦ Reducing conflict; getting along well.

- ♦ Seeing to and understanding others' needs and feelings.

Other people are basically motivated or geared toward achievements, i.e. what generically motivates or interests them relates to:

♦ Competing against challenges or standards.

♦ Attaining high levels of personal accomplishment.

♦ Reaching long term objectives (success in life).

♦ Developing new ideas and original applications.

♦ Taking calculated risks with contingency plans.

♦ Assuming responsibility for success and failure.

Lastly, other people are power-seekers, i.e. what generically motivates or interests them is what provides the chance to:

♦ Acquire reputation, status, position.

♦ Demonstrate control; lead processes.

♦ Influence others; make them follow orders.

♦ Manage, oversee, control, and teach.

♦ Avoid showing weakness.

♦ Compete.

Practical Effects

Accepting an option developed by one of the negotiation participants depends not only on the content of the proposal but also on the way and process used to materialize it. On the other hand, as mentioned earlier, in countless occasions proposals with very good content are rejected because they were inappropriately presented.

As you can imagine, when negotiating with people with different metaprograms, actions as well as the way of presenting the same idea (e.g. an option or proposal) must be different or must show varied aspects or sides to it if you wish to stir up interest in the speaker.

The same arguments that would persuade an affiliation-seeker on the importance of an option would hardly convince a power-seeker or achiever.

Useful Recommendations

a. Actions to take with affiliation-seekers.

♦ Acknowledge and underscore contributions of any idea or agreement to the group.

♦ Acknowledge the importance of social interactions and social effects of proposals.

♦ Value the importance of toning down or avoiding potential conflicts.

♦ Highlight the impact decisions will have on others.

b. Actions to be taken with achievers.

♦ Create a favorable setting to generate challenging ideas and projects.

♦ Stimulate creative thinking and initiatives.

♦ Emphasize the importance of a proposal's accuracy, planning, effectiveness and efficiency.

♦ Seek their participation in setting objectives, goals and dates.

♦ Underscore the importance of personal realization and accomplishment of specific ideas, proposals or agreements.

Actions to be taken with power-seekers.

♦ Acknowledge their status, hierarchy, position or authority.

♦ Request advice from them, recognize them (especially in public), give them credit.

♦ Provide them with symbols of power.

♦ Highlight the impact on their status and power if they accept an idea or proposal, and give them credit for it, where possible.

Easy Application

You only need a little observation and a touch of intuition to segment the majority of people you know with this tool (affiliation, power, or achievement.)

There may be a time when it is hard to classify someone, and that is perfectly reasonable. All individuals are a variable mix of the three aspects, and sometimes two of them (or all three) combine or intertwine so that it is not possible to consider one over the others. Even in such cases it seems practical to know this fact.

On the other end, there are also individuals who could be most representative of a category since they display the most salient traits of their segment or group archetypes.

However, the majority will be relatively simple to classify for they will show a clear enough main trait to understand the way they see the world; this can prove useful when negotiating.

The case of Pedro

A family-owned business —devoted to selling security systems ranging from electronic equipment to personal surveillance services— was receiving expert advice for negotiating their first generational change from the family father - about to retire- to his children, some of which served different positions in the organization.

The company was located in a large old recycled house downtown, built at the beginning of the century. One of its main architectural features - typical of the time- was the size and height of the bedrooms.

For the purpose of reducing such large spaces, the most common solutions then were building a mezzanine -height permitting-, or placing a lightweight ceiling lower than the original construction.

The office of one of the owner's sons, first-born and general manager of the company, not only was exemplary in space management creativity, but also a clear expression of one of the most salient metaprograms of the person working there. Instead of lowering the ceiling, the general manager had ordered part of the bedroom's floor to be raised; an area accessed through a semicircular staircase covered with a red carpet and furnished with an old desk and audio equipment, in addition to other furniture and office paraphernalia.

If the doors were open and the manager was in his office he was often seen working with his feet raised and heels resting on his desk. In passing, office staff would say: "There is Pedro in his throne."

In such scenario, not perceiving a possible power-seeking trait in Pedro was a deliberate effort not to see.

The answer to actions taken confirms whether you are on the right track or not when including someone in a segment. Not attaining the expected answer must lead to reviewing the form of the message conveyed or the classification made rather than interpreting it as the other side's stubbornness or obstinacy.

Is This Enough?

When negotiating, is it enough or advisable to only use a single classification mode?

Surely not. Though this classification's information is very useful for preparation and negotiation purposes, it is probably not enough to create an acceptable map (representation) of the human being's complex reality. Often, your own decisions and that of others are influenced by several metaprograms that intertwine and interrelate.

In addition to whether an individual behaves as an achiever, power-seeker or affiliation-seeker, you must ask yourself if that person is someone basically:

- A **generalist** or **detail lover?**
- **Sequential** or **random?**
- **Past, present** or **future-**oriented?
- **Impulsive, analytical** or **affective?**
- A **dreamer** (first adopter), **realist** (waits and values results) **or critic** (last adopter)?
- Preferably **visual, auditory** or **kinesthetic** to receive and process information? Believes more in what he or she sees, what is being told or what he or she experiences?
- **Avoids problems** (needs security, history, values caution and prudence) or **looks for opportunities** (possibilities and risk-taking)?
- Worries more about the **costs** of an operation or the **benefits** to be reaped?
- An **equalizer** (better reveals similarities and analogies) or a **differentiator** (perceives more differences regarding ideas and things)?
- In order to know if something is right, takes into account **inner feelings, others' opinions, statistical data**, etc.

Create a Classification Criteria List

Each can create his or her own criteria list to be applied, and when combining several classification criteria you may create a personal profile on yourself and other speakers, as suggested in Annex 1.

The following are some recommendations in this regard:

♦ Use only criteria that are useful and practical for proposed objectives.

♦ Look for simple ways, easily and quickly applicable, that enable their use even under circumstances where there is practically no time to observe or where it is impossible to ask someone to fill out the questionnaire of a complex test.

♦ Take segmentation characteristics that are easier to notice as baseline and then add others gradually, seeking to observe and picking up information from each negotiation that feeds into the new classification pattern.

♦ In some cases, when it is hard to notice patterns in one or more negotiators, ask them directly how they would like the information to be presented to them. Often, the direct way may suffice to obtain what you need.

♦ In other cases, you must use the trial and error method until you find the most appropriate one.

Persuade! This Is the Bottom Line

Persuasion has a lot to do with the negotiation content and also with understanding how people involved in the negotiation operate; how they receive and better understand the information; what information they are mostly interested in and how they filter reality and interpret it to thus create an appealing proposal, or, at least, understandable and tolerable.

A Quick Reflection

♦ If a person considers him or herself basically a generalist, how does he or she feel when a detail-lover accounts an idea, suggestion or story with full accuracy, item by item, word for word, sequentially and in an organized way?

♦ If a person considers him or herself basically a lover of details, will he or she be persuaded by someone who only gives a general view of the situation, and randomly skips from one idea to the next, sometimes without even finishing phrases or ideas?

An Illustrative Example

A recent and typical example of what we are talking about occurred with a businessman during a retreat outside the city. He and part of his team were being helped in preparing for a complex negotiation regarding a change in the management IT system of all branches of his organization. This negotiation was to be held with IT system suppliers. Once this task was completed, the consultation focused on an issue related to his technical assistant who had not been invited to participate. She was a highly skilled and reliable lady but with whom he had a hard time in almost all meetings ever since she was hired six months back.

"At times I find talking to her intolerable and nerve-racking. I don't know what's wrong with her; she's got the best credentials, and it's not a matter of disagreement on strategic decisions, nor do I dislike the quality of her work, all the contrary, her work is top quality. I really don't want to replace her; yet something is not working, it's as if we spoke different languages. I think it's a matter of chemistry," he said as we walked to the main office where his assistant's desk was.

After working with him for several days, I got to know some of his metaprograms. One of the most remarkable ones and even the one he felt most proud of, according to his own comments, was his simultaneity. In fact, when at work he was able to attend to various issues and people at a time, doing so in a scattered fashion, moving from one to the next in no given order.

Upon reaching the office and greeting his assistant I discovered right away at least one of the reasons for that "bad chemistry" between them. His assistant worked in a semi-open space close to his office, and when we walked in she was on the phone. Though she saw us come in and we greeted her she made no gesture whatsoever and continued on with her telephone conversation. When she was done with her call, she got up from her chair and greeted us very kindly; she apologized for not greeting us earlier because she was busy at the time.

"I have the impression," I said to my client, "that I already get the gist of the possible cause of the problem you pose. I think, without fear of being mistaken, that your assistant is a highly sequential and successive person in her way of working; she probably needs all task requests to be presented in a given order and step by step. She most likely can't start a new task without having first finished the previous one; and when someone unexpectedly comes in with three or four assignments —delivered all at once and, in turn, partially explained, going from one to the next- she gets upset and it feels as if she doesn't understand, or worse yet, as if she disagrees."

"That's right," he answered; "but how did you know that?"

"If you were in your assistant's shoes, what would you have done when we walked in and you were on the phone while we greeted you?"

"Ah," he said, "I would have greeted back and offered you a seat or to walk into the waiting room, and I would have even offered you a cup of coffee, all with gestures; and if you hadn't understood me I would have covered the phone with my hand and I would have said 'I'll be with you in a second, etc., etc.,"; then I would resume my conversation without a problem."

"What did you think about your assistant's attitude when we walked in?" I asked.

He replied, "Well, at that time I thought it was rude; now I think I understand what you mean", and he went on to confirm my primary diagnosis with several stories.

Lastly, we spoke about some recommendations on how to present topics, request assignments or simply communicate with his assistant in order to attain better results; and how to complement each other to become a better team, transforming the problem into an opportunity.

Shortly after, he commented not only on the excellent results obtained in his working relationship with his assistant, but also his interest in knowing more about the subject. With this technique he and his wife discovered paths to solve some of their marital difficulties.

Although most of the time there is no need to diagnose a metaprogram or classify someone in a category as a result of a single act, like in the example, sometimes that is all we have at hand.

Under normal circumstances, several of the categories mentioned earlier can help create a more complete map of the people you are negotiating with, in addition to creating a personal map that will help find a path to design proposals that adjust more to content and general interests; above all, adjusted to the way other negotiation parties process information and see the world.

Designing a map of each negotiation participant's metaprograms influences the efficiency of how other negotiation elements will be handled. In addition to:

♦ Improving communication between parties, since it points to the type of language and words to be used, as well as the conversation tone, volume or speed, and all imaginable nonverbal communication elements: from the venue where negotiations will be conducted to the appropriate dress code.

♦ Facilitating the discovery of own and counterparty's specific interests by providing a global process guideline.
♦ Making the generation of agreement options more efficient, and, above all, the way they are presented to achieve a better understanding and potential acceptance, in addition to generating more added value for ideas.
♦ Directing the search and selection of objective criteria used in order to be truly persuasive on proposal legitimacy.

Classification Criteria Map

Sequential ————————————————————————Date ——————————
Context——
Excellent criteria: _____

	0	1	2	3
Affiliation				
Power				
Achievements	_____	_____	_____	_____
Generalist						
Detail-lover				

Sequential
Random

Past
Present
Future

Dreamer
Realist
Critic

Visual
Auditory
Kinesthetic

Seeks
objectives
Avoids
problems

Equalizer
Differentiator

Self
Others
Statistics

Note: 0 to 3 identifies the degree of intensity each metaprogram presents itself with (0 means that metaprogram cannot be identified.)

- ♦ Helping to discover and gauging the value of your own options and to discover possible arguments to reduce the other side's alternatives.

- ♦ Enabling the drafting of intelligent, understandable, clear, functional and operational commitments.

- ♦ Influencing the ability to create and develop good working relationships; build trust and credibility and, in difficult, multiparty negotiations, helping towards a better and greater understanding of the complex interrelations mesh. In addition, adequately managing possible alliances and coalitions.

> *If you know the enemy and know yourself, you need not fear the result of a hundred battles. If you know yourself but not the enemy, for every victory gained you will also suffer a defeat. If you know neither the enemy nor yourself, you will succumb in every battle.*
>
> Sun Tzu

CHAPTER 3

The Loser Strategy

A Tool to Defuse Anger and Verbal
Aggression

3

Is Life a War?

It was noon; I was hungry so I went to buy something for lunch. The small supermarket close to my office was fine to buy a light snack. On my way past the grocer's I got tempted by some apples. As usual, I decided to squeeze one and see if it was right for my taste. I didn't quite like or dislike how it felt so I decided to delay my purchase decision. I then walked into the supermarket, bought my lunch and when I got to the cash register to pay, I noticed the grocer waiting for me, clearly upset, holding an apple.

"Did you walk in and squeeze an apple?" he asked in a serious tone and evidently disturbed.

"Yes I did," I replied.

"Look what you've done."

The apple had a small dent, and, surely too, my fingerprints.

"If every person who walked in did that, can you imagine how the apples would look like? I won't be able to sell *this* one. What do you say?"

"You are right," I said nicely. "Sell me the apple."

His first reaction was that of surprise. He didn't know what to do for a few seconds and then went on to say, switching his tone of voice: "No, please, I didn't mean you should buy it; I just wanted to explain the situation to you."

"I understand what you're saying," I answered, "and you are right. Please sell me the apple."

"No, I don't want to sell it to you," he insisted and walked out of the store. I paid the bill and left.

I tried once again and this time I said: "Please, sell me an apple."

"No, that wasn't my intention," said the grocer, and added in a cordial tone. "I only wanted…"

"I know, but won't you sell me an apple? I want one."

"All right," he said, "my treat." He put the apple in a bag, gave it to me and shook my hand.

We greeted each other goodbye; I thanked him and walked away determined to write this chapter.

The Loser Strategy

> *Here I discovered a new and deeper understanding of a wonderfully beautiful Evangelical maxim yet frequently ill interpreted. Till then it had unleashed contradictory feelings: If someone slaps you on one cheek turn the other one toward him.*
>
> *A wolf has taught me: You must turn the other cheek to your enemy not to be hurt again but to make it impossible for him to go on hurting you.*

Konrad Lorenz, Noble Prize in Medicine, 1973

Professor Rodolfo Talice, a prominent Uruguayan scientist who has published over 30 books (16 on ethology) states that wolves, dogs, geese, monkeys and almost all animal species use the so-called 'loser strategy' to contain the attack of the most powerful opponents. A small gesture, sometimes exposing the neck, at others lowering the head or tail, and perhaps a subtle smell of humans may automatically trigger this mechanism. Professor Talice tells, for example, that when two wolves are fighting to defend their status in the pack and one of them feels that mortal defeat, it exposes its neck to its opponent.

Such behavior, far from provoking the attack from the strongest, forces it to stop the fight.

The key question and perhaps hard to answer is: regardless of appearances, which of the two opponents assumed leadership and controlled the desperate situation?

The paradox of such behavior underpinning this strategy is to initially trigger confusion, and then comes the unexpected reaction given the circumstances: he who has power over life and death halts.

Based on these facts Lorenz uses great wit to reflect upon the real meaning of the Biblical passage:

> *"You have heard that it was said: 'Eye for eye, tooth for tooth.'*
> *But I tell you, do not resist an evil person. If anyone slaps you on the*
> *right cheek, turn to them the other cheek also. And if anyone wants to*
> *sue you and take your shirt, hand over your cloak as well. If anyone*
> *forces you to go one mile, go with them two miles."*

Mathew 5: 38-41

This behavior seems to be built into the genetics of many animals and the result of the strategy is almost unfailing in 100% of cases and under natural conditions. "Under natural conditions" entails life developed in a natural **habitat**, since for example, rabbits living in captivity can fight each other to death.

Contrary to animals, humans do not seem to have that trigger mechanism genetically built-in. They are able to show, even under conditions of surrender to the opponent, escalating feelings of anger and behavior such as savageness and sadism. It has been evidenced by World War II calamities. However, this clarification is helpful to appreciate that applying the strategy will not guarantee –as with inferior animals– sure success in all cases; it is important to underscore its value to defuse verbal aggression in human conflicts starting from every day controversies to more complex forms.

The Strategy in Action

Though Christ seems to have drawn a teaching from this strategy, chances are it must have been used intuitively before and certainly afterwards.

It can be identified at the heart of the behavior and moves of leaders who have overcome by using and recommending passive resistance, such as Gandhi, to mention an example.

In these cases, what has stopped powerful adversaries when faced with defenseless people? Without a doubt, overt helplessness is the source of power. Companies and labor unions also know the strength of helplessness.

The paradoxical behavior of working to rule, i.e. obeying each and every rule to the fullest extent, without offering apparent resistance to rule books, is based on this strategy as a leadership and control tool for those who do not hold the power.

What about some Japanese companies where workers on strike produce more; or hunger strikes as a way of getting what you want from an extremely weak position?

What seems to work in large human and organizational movements also works in everyday life. What do you think happens in a household when a flower vase breaks, anger ensues, and there appears a little fellow with a ball under his arms, looking down and says: "Daddy, it was me, I'm sorry." A typical answer to such behavior may be complimenting him for his courage and honesty in admitting the fact, rather than punishing him.

How many times does a simple apology for a poor traffic maneuver instantly defuse an angry driver? Where could a scene like this end up if not mediated by that small gesture (expression of a refined strategy)?

The answer is well-known by all.

Psychological Foundations

According to experts, human beings do not seem to have this survival mechanism genetically ingrained. This article proves it and suggests using it more often.

Yet, to a greater or lesser extent, the majority of individuals include this strategy of control of the strongest and most powerful during the first years of their lives. Lowering the head like some animals do is a familiar gesture for humans, like children's attitude when being reprimanded.

We have been taught not to take advantage of the helpless under the form of clear rules of good upbringing and politeness, for example in public transport when giving up the seat to the elderly, disabled or a pregnant woman. Moral norms arising from heroes' attitudes ("Mercy to the defeated", Jose Artigas, Battle of *Las Piedras*, May 18, 1811) convey the same message.

At other times, in a concealed way, parents, mothers or other people manipulate and sometimes intimidate in their role as victims when realizing intuitively how much more powerful their apparent destitution is than shouting or threatening with punishment to stop undesired behavior.

To most people this type of programming prevents them from feeling the pleasure of insulting, having the upper hand or benefiting vis-à-vis someone who is defenseless or hopeless. On the contrary, the majority of people would feel guilty or remorseful, and it is unlikely that anyone could feel like a winner under those circumstances.

Symmetry and Complementarity

These concepts were originally introduced in 1935 by Bateson who basically establishes that interrelations between two individuals (or even between two nations) can be symmetrical or complementary.

Symmetrical is the relationship based on equality where each individual's behavior is like the reflection of the other.

Complementary is the relationship based on differences where each individual's behavior is distinct from each other. In this case, there are two positions, namely, superior or one-up and inferior or one-down.

None of these interrelation types bear any positive or negative, good or bad, powerful or weak, appropriate or inappropriate connotation per se in a given situation.

A symmetrical interrelation may be appropriate if, for example, both persons express care, appreciation or acknowledgment towards each other. The negative aspect of symmetry is seen in the so-called symmetrical escalation, where the insult or aggression of one party is followed by a greater insult or aggression from the other; or the arms race of a nation is followed by another arms race from its adversary.

Likewise, a complementary relationship may be appropriate and totally common like mother and baby or teacher and student. The negative side of complementarity is crystallization; for example, when a mother is unable to recognize that her child has grown enough to develop a relationship of equality (symmetrical) in several aspects of life.

The solution to many interrelation problems in negotiations and everyday life may arise from applying the simple rule of introducing symmetry into complementarity and complementarity into symmetry.

Evidently, the loser strategy is based on introducing complementarity into symmetry or symmetric escalation situations. The user assumes a position of inferiority or one-down which has nothing to do with weakness or strength, adequacy or inadequacy, good or bad, nor does it define who is eventually right.

A Practical Guide

"The supreme art of war is to subdue the enemy without fighting…"
"To take what you attack, attack the unprotected."

Sun Tzu. 4th century B.C.

Four centuries before Christ, this Chinese general innovated on how to view armed confrontations inasmuch as he did not recognize in great battlefield killings the highest expression of the strategy, rather, all to the contrary, in the paradoxical way of acting which is summed up in the first quote: "Subdue without fighting." Differences aside, what is contradictory about the loser strategy is the core of its power.

First Things First: Define the Objective

Like in other life situations, when confronted with verbal aggression (ideas), successful people know how to distinguish what is relevant in order to focus all efforts there.

Often, those that are verbally attacked pay attention to the content of the aggression to try to counter argue; this accounts for a strategic error: "Attack where the enemy is unprotected." This counter argument is often perceived by the opponent as a counterattack which creates conflict escalation.

Those who act in this way fuel the conflict and lose sight of what is relevant: to manage the anger and emotion of the other side. If anger is not defused, you will most likely be unable to discuss content.

Attack Where the Enemy is Unprotected

The person who verbally attacks often expects the attacked one to defend him or herself counter attacking on the content. Paradoxically, what the attacker does not expect is this not to happen.

In the example of my friend, the grocer, as must have been the case in other occasions, what he probably expected me to say could have been as follows:

"It wasn't me, I touched the apple but I didn't squeeze it. How do you know *that* was the apple I touched? Hey, listen, it was nothing. What does it matter, you will sell it anyway to someone. Turn the bruised side down and that's it"; or any other counter-argument. I need not explain what would have happened then.

On the contrary, what changed matters was that, like in judo or aikido, I aligned myself with his energy to change its direction.

"You are right," I said and, just like a wolf exposes its neck to the other, at first I noticed confusion on his face and then, towards the end, he became pleasant as a result of my gesture. He was evidently not prepared for that. Like Eastern martial arts what astonishes is the apparent paradox enclosed in actions and there, too, lies the power.

In summary, if during a negotiation a situation ensues where symmetrical escalation is bound to happen, the recommendation is not to insist on the cause of controversy, leave the circle and seek to restore adequate communication and working relationship to later resume the elements of substance (interests, options and legitimacy criteria.)

In many cases, the loser strategy will prove a useful tool to achieve this goal in negotiation.

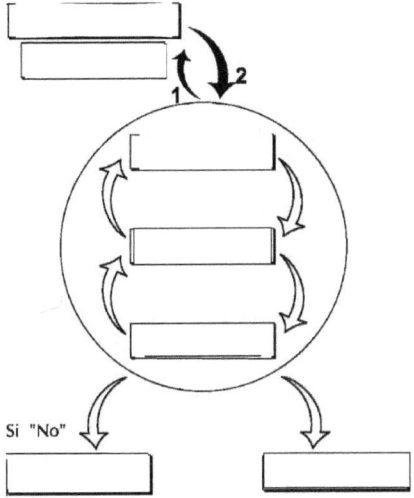

Some Final Recommendations

When you are certain that what the angry speaker is saying is true, the magic words are: "You are right."

In other cases, when you are not so sure, statements like:

"You are probably right", "It is possible that you are right",

"Perhaps you are right", if appropriately expressed, may have the same effect and at the same time leave room for other possibilities.

The expression "You are probably right" includes many other options to look at the same fact, as well as the possibility of its opposite (you are probably wrong.)

What determines success in such cases is the honesty with which such sentences are uttered. When said ironically, with sarcasm, or just inconsistently they cannot be a part of this strategy and do not work.

So, how do you solve situations where it is simply impossible to align with anything the opponent says and his or her critique or aggression is considered unjustified?

This often occurs at the claims section in stores: A lady bought a home appliance a few days ago and approaches the counter; she is very angry and criticizes the device (it does not work), the store and the salesperson. She does not state clearly what happened, only that it is broken; she pounds on the counter, raises her voice and demands her money back.

If you are in the salesperson's shoes, without further information, it is hard to honestly agree with the content of the complaint and tell the customer she is right. In such case, if you are unable to align with what the other person is saying, we suggest you do it with emotions.

You will always be on the right side if you say something along these lines: "I understand how you feel, if I had bought an appliance I needed and two days later it stopped working, I would feel just like you" (which is not to say that I might act differently.) In summary, it is like saying: "If I were you I'd feel just the way you do." A safer version on account of its absolute theoretical certainty is: "If I were you, I would surely feel the same" (and nobody can deny it.)

PACING - ALIGNING: "I understand how you feel."

LEADING - REDIRECTING: "Let me see what I can do for you."

None of these expressions say anything about claim acceptance or the customer's initial proposal, nor does it include any compromise. It just enables anger to be defused in order to begin a dialogue; pacing to later lead. They seek to resume appropriate communication and relationship to allow for assertive discussion of substantive issues (interests, options and legitimacy criteria.)

The following question often arises in these cases: What to do when the person is so angry there is no room for dialogue?

The suggestion is: «let off some steam before opening the lid», that is, allow the other to vent a little and calm down. When that is achieved you can resume the strategy. Do not forget some people are very irritable and stubborn and they will need several doses.

Sometimes you might ask yourself: And if that doesn't work either?

In that case, you must resort to a different strategy.

More than just a rhetorical artifact, the loser strategy is one of the subtlest ways of power and leadership. If it can save some animal lives, it may occasionally save human lives. Less dramatically, when used wisely it may save an important negotiation, a company, a job, a family, a couple or friendship. In short, it is a subtle form of power and a superb tool to restore communication and working relationships in negotiations.

> *"There are cases where achieving a goal is only possible under cordial terms and not through violence even when resorted to."*

"Kalilah and Dimnah" Baidaba. 6th century BC.

CHAPTER 4

Did You Get It? Nooooo!

Linguistic Meta Model: A Tool That Helps Reduce Misunderstandings and Confusion

4

At some point in a negotiation every person has probably heard something like this:

"Listen, I only want justice to be done!"

Now, what is the answer to the question "What does justice mean?"

The only valid answer is: Justice for whom?

Words are void of meaning especially the most abstract ones. The meaning of a word, what it stands for, depends on the recipient or the user as well as on the form or context where used.

When communicating during the course of negotiations or your daily life, there is no guarantee that the meaning of words used will be the same for all persons involved in the process, especially when dealing not with simple words but rather complex phrases. As you may well imagine, it is an endless source of misunderstandings oftentimes resulting from the delusion of having understood.

In a Latin American country, several women's organizations pointed out that the government was not complying with the duty agreed to with their organizations. On the other hand, the government claimed they had fulfilled their promise. The whole discussion revolved around a sentence in the agreement signed some time back which clearly stated as follows: The government is committed to encouraging the national women's forum.

Once again, it is legitimate to ask: What is the meaning of encourage? What is understood by encourage? What did women's organizations and what did the government understand when they signed the agreement?

Diagnosis: There was a delusion and consequently a fuzzy commitment which is the source of new conflicts.

Many negotiations fail during or after signing an agreement because, like in the previous example, its participants fail to understand or believe all is clear when in reality it was just an illusion.

Nothing New Under the Sun

Perhaps the first reflections on the subject in the Western culture date back to the 5th century B.C., in Socrates' Greece.

The Greek sophist Gorgias at the time used to say with great clarity: "Language is not reality. Words respond to the opinion, notion, belief or way of perceiving reality by the speaker, and, most likely, differ from that of recipients. Reality and language are two distinct things since nothing real can become words and vice versa."

Much later, Alfred Korzybski coined the happy expression: "The map is not the territory it represents," and like Gorgias, says: "The word is not the thing it denotes. The word apple is not an apple; it is only a representation of an apple."

Similar to what a computer does when a fact is perceived through the senses; the brain creates the representation of a multidimensional reality encompassing space, time and color, etc. known as a mental map.

When it was built it had to go through various filters and processes and so such representation is far from reality itself, just like a map is different from the territory it represents.

Creating Mental Maps

In the process of mind mapping your senses are a first limiting factor; though enabling information on the reality to be captured they are in and of themselves a filter of such reality. Although very well equipped as a whole, there are countless elements in reality that human senses are unable to perceive. For example, certain light or sound wave lengths go absolutely unnoticed to the human eye or ear needing some instruments to detect them; whereas, under the same circumstances, certain animals could do so naturally in some cases, e.g. the sound of a dog whistle.

♦ Human beings use a set of processes for mind mapping thus called universal processes for model creation. All people delete, distort or generalize things from reality.

a. Deletion: The process whereby you selectively focus on part of the experience blocking out other existing parts. Till this moment, you probably had no idea about the amount of saliva in your mouth or how your feet are resting on the floor. Nevertheless, now we also know such data was there and available, simply blocked and deleted because attention was being paid to reading.

a. Distortion: The process that allows modifying data in the reality perceived by senses. Fantasy, creativity, novels, works of art of many great painters or sculptors are examples of this process.

b. Generalization: The process whereby a fact, event or element (or a few) is taken as representative of the whole category yet being only a specific example.

♦ It is interesting because although all people use these processes they do so differently given the same set of circumstances. They delete different things, distort distinct elements and generalize facts differently; so it is easy to understand that taking into account the same reality, representations different people have of that reality may be infinite. Previous education, maps and programs, the culture we live in, the family we belong to, our schooling and professional training shape processes, and to a certain extent dictate, within a greatly complex reality, what things we pay attention to, what we will or will not perceive, how we build generalizations and how we distort. For example, the skills an Eskimo has to perceive and distinguish subtle differences in ice have little to do with the skills of an individual born in the Caribbean. Surely this situation would be the exact opposite if we spoke of fruit. Even those who live under the influence of the same culture and family experience differently or live their experiences in a particular way; this determines their own life story and unique traits when creating maps and representations of reality.

Human Communication Is a Miracle

Many might think that if human communication does exist it is a miracle since, to complicate matters further, being and appearing get confused. Something that is perceived or appears to be a certain way gets confused with reality although it truthfully is not.

This implies that all possible ways of perceiving the world are valid hence making all things relative.

> *Things are to me as they appear to me, and are to you as they*
> *appear to you, you and I being men.*

Plato

However, social coexistence is possible for humans because as they belong to the same society, group or family they share (at least partly) a set of maps, probably because processes and how to create them have been learned from within the group itself.

The Power of Words

> *The word has an enormous power. A word has such a small body and*
> *may exert enormous power to stop fear and remove sorrow, and to create*
> *joy and augment pity.*
> Gorgias

Words are one of the most common and important ways to represent reality and create mental maps. In fact, each word is a map and sentences built with words are simply more complex maps.

Linguists call the way we typically speak 'superficial structure of language' resulting from deep structures of the language, i.e. linguistic structures most complete and closest to the best representation of a fact though differing from it.

The processes whereby deep structures change into superficial ones are called transformations (hence transformational grammar.)

To illustrate the above:

Real world	→	Universal filters and processes	→	Original representation: Images Sounds Emotions Sensations	→	Deep linguistic representation ↑ Transformational grammar	→	Superficial linguistic representation

Beyond the difficulties mentioned earlier regarding mind mapping, it is clear that the transformation process often adds an additional complication. Typically, the most common form of expression is a poor and distorted version of a richer representation stored in our brain.

When negotiating, like in so many other activities in life, it is of paramount importance to clearly know what the other person means when articulating "X".

In some negotiations it is essential to be able to inquire on a fact or idea when searching for the other side's best map.

So it is critical to have a tool to enable the process of a systematic search for more complete meanings and representations of the other side's expressions which, in turn, helps for applying to our own expressions, where possible and convenient.

A Light at the End of the Tunnel

Recently, Richard Bandler and John Grinder created a guide on how language works and how to resolve problems created in communication when representations of the reality (words themselves) mean different things to different people; or when given the same reality, different individuals create distinct representations. This tool allows for the discovery of new data that helps in creating more complete and adjusted maps.

The guide was called *Linguistic Meta Model*, a model of models, a map on how to use language. The meta model helps connect language once again to the representation of an experience and understand the meaning of each articulation, thus adding sense to the communication.

John Grinder created a simplified version that allows for a more practical approach to the problem of really knowing what the other person means when uttering "X".

Grinder's version is one of the simplest and most powerful tools at the service of one of the key elements in negotiation: good communication.

In order to understand – critical for persuasion– it is necessary to find within relevant information the meaning and wealth lost in superficial language.

The instrument the meta model uses for that purpose is the same one Socrates used circa 2500 years ago: the question.

When, How and What to Ask

Although the number of possible transformations is greater than the one presented here, the following five are a simplified and highly efficient version to get started.

Each transformation will be followed by a brief definition, an example, the clarification of its objective, and, too, some reference will be provided on the type of question for assistance purposes.

1. Unspecified nouns

   Definition: The object or noun is not specified in the sentence.
   Example: They scare me.

   Objective: to clarify specifically to whom reference is made.

   Question: Who specifically scares you? Key words: they, them, some, etc. NOTE: This applies equally to terms such as justice, equity, productivity, happiness, acknowledgment, and many others that may lead to different interpretations. The goal is to determine which interpretation the speaker refers to. In doing so it is important to ask: "What specifically are you referring to when you say…?", or "What specifically do you understand by…?"

2. Unspecified verbs

   Definition: Details are not provided on how something was (or will be) done or said.
   Example: I will settle this issue.

Objective: to define details about the "how".

Question: How will it specifically be done?

1. Comparisons without referents

    Definition: Something being compared to which is missing in the sentence.

    Example: "In this kind of negotiations it is best to play tough."

    Objective: to recover the comparison element and criterion.

    Question: "Better than what, or compared specifically to what?" Key words: better, worse, the most [...], the least [...], greater, smaller, etc.

    NOTE: Much in keeping with comparisons without referents are judgments about someone or something without mentioning who makes them and based on what rationale.

    Example: "Clearly, this is not the right way to act in this case."

    Objective: to identify who passes judgment, and criteria used.

    Question: "Evident to whom?" "Correct to whom specifically?" "Based on what criteria?"

    Key words: pay special attention to adverbs ending in "ly". Evidently, clearly, obviously, consequently, etc. which are used to remove the person passing judgment.

2. Universal quantifiers

    Definition: It relates to very broad generalizations.

    Example: "I've never done well in business."

    Objective: to discover a generalization's exception or counterexample.

    Question: "Never ever?" "There was never an instance you did well in business?"

    Another way is to discover which specifically was the experience that gave rise to the generalization: "In which instance specifically did you not do well?" "What situation are you referring to?"

    Key words: never, always, all, none, ever, etc.

3. Modal Operators (MO) of Necessity and Possibility

    Definition: Terms that reveal thought and behavior-limiting rules or standards.

    Example of Modal Operator of Necessity (MON): "Nobody should be trusted in a negotiation."

    Example of Modal Operator of Possibility (MOP): "I can't find interests underlying positions."

    Objective of MON: to defy the limitation by identifying the consequences of not abiding by the rule.
    Objective of MOP: to discover the cause.

    Question for MON: "What if I trusted?"

    Question for MOP: "What prevents me from doing so?"

Key words for MON: "must", "should", "have to", "need to", etc.

TRANSGRESSION	QUESTION
Unspecified noun	How does that specifically happen?
Unspecified verbs - Comparisons	Compared to what?
Universal Quantifiers	Never? Always? In which case...?
Judgments	Who says...? Based on what...?
Modal Operators of Necessity	What if...?
Modal Operators of Possibility	What prevents you from...?
What or who specifically...?	
(See Annex 1)	

Table 4—1 What and how to ask.

When and How to Ask

The Meta Model, as well as this simplified version, is a powerful tool provided that, like any other tool, it is correctly used. An incorrect use of the Meta Model means:

1. Asking questions when the answer is not relevant to the goals of conversation or the negotiation as a whole.

2. Using an inappropriate tone when asking questions making the other person feel intimidated.

On the contrary, it is advisable:

♦ To ask provided that the data sought is relevant or useful to understand or help others understand what the counterpart thinks when articulated. Like all skills and unlike techniques, this one is not easily conveyed. Knowing when and in what situation it is relevant to ask in the course of a negotiation is highly variable, contextual and subjective.

♦ You will save time if you can identify and clarify unspecified nouns early on. Then, seek to clarify the remaining transgressions.

♦ Use mitigating phrases like: "I was wondering", "I would like to know ", "I'm curious about"... "This is very interesting and I wonder ...?" "Let me see if I understood correctly."

♦ To add in all cases a tone of healthy curiosity when posing questions.

If you address these details you will acquire one of the most powerful tools for understanding. If used inappropriately it may lead not only to a failed negotiation but also to worsening the future relationship with your counterparty.

Why Is the Question "Why" Missing?

You may have noticed that neither the original Meta Model version nor this simplified one has included the question "Why?" Though this question should not be forbidden, oftentimes when somebody uses it during negotiations it only results in vague answers and generalizations or justifications of the fact or expression that gave rise to the question, thus barely useful to improve understanding. For example: "Why do you say I'm unfair?" "Because so, you are."

Given that this question aims at the past it may often sound inquisitive, so it should be used carefully and together with nonverbal communication expressing real annoyance. When wanting to know the reason for something a good substitute is "what for?" since it is directed to the future and the answer typically helps to better understand a fact or expression.

> *"He who dominates speech (rhetoric) dominates the mind and soul of people."*
>
> Gorgias

Other transgressions	Annex 1
Simple deletion ♦ I am worried.	Question: "About what specifically?"
Nominalizations ♦ We must deal with this assertively.	Question: "Who must be assertive and with whom or what specifically?"
Judgments, judge or criterion ♦ Clearly, that's not the right way to go about it.	Questions: "Evident to whom?" "Right for whom?" "Based on what criteria specifically?"
Assumptions ♦ If he or she knew the importance of good communication in negotiating he or she wouldn't act that way.	Questions: "What makes you think your interlocutor doesn't know it?" "How do you know he or she doesn't know it?" "How specifically is he or she acting?"
Cause-effect ♦ Your questions make me nervous.	Question: "Specifically, how do they do it?"
Mind reading ♦ I know exactly what makes you act this way.	Question: "Specifically, how do they know?"
Complex equivalent ♦ Instead of paying attention to me you are scribbling.	Question: "How do you know that scribbling specifically means that no attention is being paid?"

CHAPTER 5

Who Is in Charge
in This Negotiation?

5

Two-party Negotiation; Multi-party Negotiation

My wife –also a doctor– and I share the same office space: an old recycled house in the neighborhood of Pocitos, in Montevideo.

When we decided to move from the previous house we wanted something similar but more spacious. We asked a friend of ours who is the owner of a real estate agency to help us in our search.

A couple of days later, he showed us a house located two blocks away from ours that belonged to a Uruguayan painter who had recently passed away. The house was undergoing settlement of estate proceedings between nine heirs who lived in different countries: some in Uruguay, others in Brazil, yet others in the United States and, lastly, some in Israel.

It was a two-story house with a beautiful façade which was accessed through a very large, semicircular-arched iron and glass gate overlooking the garage.

Once past the gate, the entrance to the house was through a door on one of the garage's side walls. The opposite wall was fully covered by a mural created by the artist made of small colored mosaics.

I am no expert in art or murals and my first impression was horrendous; so much so that I immediately thought if we were to buy the house the first thing I would do was get rid of the mural.

We walked through the house and it was really beautiful and also matched all our needs in terms of size, circulation, etc.

Since we had already been researching the market we decided to make an offer which my friend would negotiate with the heirs.

A few days later, I got a call from the agency saying that things were looking good and that several of the more influential heirs consulted agreed on the price and payment method.

My friend called me up again two days later saying that one of the heirs had requested the removal of the garage mural in an effort to sell it to the electric service provider's (UTE) amusement park for which the painter had already performed some artwork.

My almost immediate answer was: "NO, no way, tell them NO. Tell them I went to see the house with the mural on the wall and so it is included in the deal. Are they crazy? Next thing you know they'll want to take the toilet seat and sell it because that's where the artist sat. Tell them NO, it is a definite NO."

A long silence ensued on the other side of the line and there followed my friend's calm voice saying —knowing my previous opinion on the mural: "Julio, let's be reasonable, if the mural were worth a sizeable amount they wouldn't leave it; they'd just not cut a deal with you, take down the mural and then put the house up for sale again. If the mural is worthless, why worry? And the bottom line is: What business are you in anyway? Why *are* you buying a new house? What's your real interest in moving? Are you now in the business of buying and selling murals and paintings?"

At that point, besides blushing, two important memories came to mind.

First I remembered Roger Fisher constantly advising his students and clients to focus on interests not positions. He also mentioned, even knowing this rule, the ease with which you may fall into the trap of doing the opposite in the course of a negotiation.

The second thing I remembered was the origin of the psychological current created by the psychiatrist Doctor Eric Berne and introduced into Latin America and Spain by Doctor Roberto Kertesz.

Berne has psychoanalytic training and started developing his brilliant theory while working with a patient, Ned, a 35-year-old lawyer.

At times, Ned behaved like an efficient and rational practitioner and was able to make important decisions; at others, he did so like a child, reluctant to face trials out of fear. He would get drunk and high all alone in his cabin in the countryside surrounded by weapons and porn magazines. Both patient and therapist perceived this.

Ned said: "That is exactly how I feel sometimes... That I'm not really a lawyer but a child."

Berne commented in one of his articles: "Everything that was spoken to this patient was heard by two people: the adult lawyer and the child [...] One part rationally managed reality and the other did so archaically [...] It was apparent there existed two states of the ego, both for the patient and the observer: one of an adult and another of a child."

Berne noticed that depending on how he approached Ned, he obtained either of both behaviors. He decided to call the rational ego state of the lawyer « (A) Adult » and the child ego state «(C) Child».

In the course of negotiations, I often find myself watching and listening to important and adult individuals negotiating like children.

At times, though negotiating over millions of dollars, participants are involved in children's games and behave as such, handling reality through their childish programs although rational-looking.

We have all learned to negotiate ever since childhood and we did so the best way we could which by no means is a sin. What *can* be considered a sin is to continue using the same tactics and automatic answers in our adult life, especially in circumstances that call for more than just kicking or screaming.

An Unbeatable Trio

Upon examining Ned further, Berne discovered behaviors that did not quite match any of the two previously described ego states. Some of those behaviors resembled behaviors of one of the lawyer's parents, so he called this third ego state, Ned's third program, this third disguise: « (P) Parent ».

According to the ego state in control of the situation, Ned displayed very distinct behaviors.

Thus Ned could sometimes speak of generous handling of money like his father would have done; at others, how to make cold and calculating adult decisions on investment; and at other occasions be concerned like a child for pennies spent.

So Berne described each ego state as «a system of consistent thoughts and feelings directly relating to corresponding consistent patterns of behavior. »

If we resembled our brain to a computer we could then imagine three great sections of data and program files which, aligned to Berne's thinking, we will call: (P) Parent, (A) Adult and (C) Child, and, as Berne, we will illustrate them with three stacked circles.

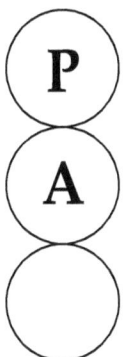

In the (P) Parent file *what must and must not be done ... the learned sense of life* is pre-recorded. It contains files on culture, traditions, values, all types of rules, prejudices and preconceptions we have about things and people and what is moral and not. If these are the programs that are in control at a given time, our behavior patterns will be similar to those of any influential parental figure during our childhood or teenage years (father, mother, older siblings, tutors, grandparents, teachers, etc.)

From that particular ego state we judge, give orders, critique or protect others or ourselves as our parents would; what used to be external is now within.

When we are very young and our adult state still not well developed to screen information and decide what is or not convenient to store, our recordings are direct, without analyzing their usefulness, trueness, accuracy or practicality.

The pattern of those unexamined recordings is to make us repeat or copy others' behaviors.

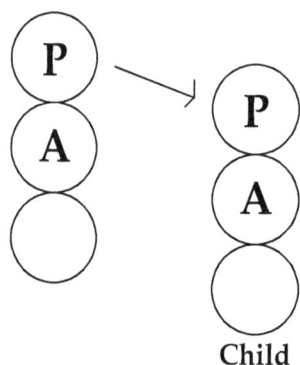

Child

"Never give in, you'll be deemed weak."

Another way of adding information to that file is through the Adult filter.

When this other part of the computer is well-developed it may assess whether parental messages received are appropriate and convenient for filing, or may even draw own conclusions on facts and create new rules; alter or rule out others previously filed.

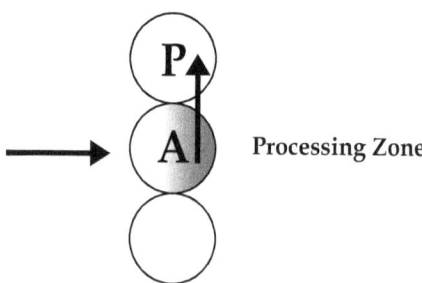

Processing Zone

Nevertheless, changing parental recordings, prejudices and preconceptions is not as easy as you might imagine.

Firstly, they occur unnoticed, and secondly, when someone questions any of those pre-recordings it creates resistance and all kinds of strong feelings in individuals, families, companies, communities or nations.

Although widely accepted that parental recordings cannot be erased, it is also known that they could be transferred to «dead files» or updated by the Adult.

The (A) Adult ego state starts developing from age two in life and becomes stronger through use and appropriate stimulation. It is that part of our computer which is responsible for reasoning and dictating *what should or should not* be done. It draws data from reality, collects external and internal information (from its own file and other computer parts), logically processes and organizes that data to decide on the most appropriate response for future execution from any other ego state.

It analyzes and measures the potential consequences of a variety of decisions. That is where dispassionate scientific thinking and our programs are filed, whether good or bad, for rational decision-making and problem solving.

Like any other computer, in addition to the quality of programs used, the output will depend on the quality of input material; it is hence easy to predict that if this part uses data acquired from the other two files the results of its processes will also be impacted by the quality of files there stored.

When the (C) Child in our computer is in control of our actions we feel, sense, create, think, are moved and act like when we were kids. That is where *our likes, dislikes, sense of life notion* and biological matters are filed (gender, color of the iris or skin, size, etc.) That is where we bring in all magical thoughts, the irrational, superstition, curiosity, intuition, creativity, overall grasping of ideas or situations, as well as the perception of subtle meanings of nonverbal messages (body language, voice tones, etc.) According to my teacher, Doctor Roberto Kertesz, therein lies the best and worst of each of us.

In any circumstance, including our negotiations, the three ego states or computer parts can work together in coordination to attain, like in a music trio, the best melody and best possible results.

Any stimulus may also eventually be resolved by using the skills and programs of a single ego state.

Results will vary between excellent to catastrophic depending not only on file content and program quality but also on resource adequacy and coordination (ego state or computer part), as required.

In the story described at the beginning of this chapter, the lack of well-coordinated ego states was evident, to say the least. What started off as a negotiation from an Adult ego state, no longer worked in different occasions when faced with a variety of stimuli.

When in your Parent Ego state				
	Subjective		Objective	
	I think	I feel	I say	I do
PARENT (What you *must* do: prejudices)	The young are very impulsive and immature to negotiate with.	Sympathy	You are too young and inexperienced to understand what's convenient for you.	Overprotective tone. Hand on the shoulder.
	You must be hard when negotiating	Anger.	I don't have much time. Stick to the point, take it or leave it.	Looks at the watch.
	Everyone is equal when negotiating. If you turn your back you're dead.	Outrage.	What are you up to with your proposal?	Judgmental look and finger-pointing.

ADULT (What is most convenient, collecting data from reality: estimating probabilities)	I don't understand why you're so angry. This is a question of numbers.	Nothing	I insist, what's important are numbers and what numbers say.	Robotic repetition. Cold tone.
	I'm being threatened with the alternative. I should change the game.		How can negotiating with them suit your interests better than negotiating with us? Tell me about your interests.	Stands up to write on the flipchart.
	Tries to manipulate mixing relationship with the substance.		It is best to separate what each one feels from what I deserve based on the data and results.	Gesture of separating hands and going back to taking down notes on numbers. Laughs.
CHILD (What you like doing: emotions, physical feelings, creativity, irrational ideas.)	I'm going to make him lose control and see what happens. After all…	Triumphalism	What you're saying is funny, it's crazy…	Sweat on hands and forehead. Blushes.
	Negotiating makes me nervous: especially on a Friday.	Fear. Anxiety	Umm; the thing is ummm… Well, ahem. Yeees… I don't know…	Rubs hands.
	Today is my day.	Elation	Don't talk to me about alternatives, this is great business!	

Let's consider the first example: when I irrationally decided to get rid of the mural just because I disliked it (C) without considering its economic value (A) or aesthetic or emotional value to others (P), or the ulterior consequences of removing it altogether.

Second behavior: my whimsical reaction to the mural removal request. In that instance, putting core negotiation interests at risk I downright answered "NO", acting like a spoilt child when someone takes away a useless toy he wasn't even playing with.

Who Should "Play" in My Negotiations?

Obviously a good negotiation benefits from using all our ego states, in harmony and coordination, sequentially appearing at distinct negotiation stages according to the type of situation we are undergoing, and also depending on the negotiator(s) we are dealing with.

Overall, a good result for the preparation, negotiation or assessment stages requires –preferably in both negotiators– *a good adult* handling *a good method* in order to timely coordinate the participation of the other ego states, just like a good orchestra director does with various instruments.

A suitable Parent ego state will contribute and respect those values that create trust and credibility —enabling conditions to achieve a good setting and *working relationship.* That ego state will safeguard mutual benefits and help sustain *legitimacy criteria,* objective standards and data unrelated to Child whims hence enabling assertive problem solving. It will help the Adult and Child accept what is legitimate and fair, even when arising from the opposite side, and will seek a good negotiation outcome where all parties feel equally treated and none cheated. It will suggest procedural rules, allowing for and encouraging creativity for each party's Child to be reflected through the creation of multiple options with good value added.

An adequate Adult ego state will establish the best preparation methods and tools, the most convenient negotiation strategies and agenda as well as tools for result assessment. Before starting the negotiation, the Adult ego state will enable agreements with the other side on the applicability and convenience of rules suggested by the Parent ego state on how the negotiation will take place. It will help the Child explore and discover the real *interests* underlying positions and search for the best way to appropriately articulate them. It will clarify all *communication* uncertainties by presenting, listening to and posing smart questions to understand, and, in turn, be understood. It will assess pros and cons of each *option* on the negotiation table to satisfy interests, and separate the typical invention process in the Child from decision-making in the Adult ego state realm. It will explore and compare walk-away *alternatives* to satisfy interests, and based on these and objective standards will decide on limitations to the case. It will be the ultimate decision maker, checking on the Child's likes and on the Parent regarding what should be done and what is most convenient given the case.

It will ultimately decide whether it is best to accept one of the options and establish an *agreement* or stop negotiating and consider the best alternative to a negotiated agreement (BATNA). It will also make sure, if agreement is reached, that it be intelligent, i.e. realistic, operational and functional. Once the negotiation is over, it will assess results, draw own conclusions about what did work and what is advisable to repeat under similar conditions, and what could be done differently, as well as motives for acting so.

If possible, it will create new rules, criteria and generalizations with those conclusions that could be filed with the Parent to be used under similar circumstances without need to repeat the process. It will update some Parent rules, so what is considered objective criteria today may simply be prejudices in the future.

A suitable Child ego state will contribute the nuts and bolts of the negotiation: its fears, worries, wishes, dreams and desires which under the Adult command will become negotiation interests, goals and objectives. It accounts for all the creativity and innovative freedom when generating value-added options leaving nothing behind or money on the table. It is worth clarifying that when using the term "value-added" we are not referring only to its materialistic sense, though sometimes we metaphorically say "not leaving money on the table". We rather refer to the notion that complex negotiations must go beyond simple bargaining; the «win-win» concept does not stand for just money but also the pursuit of options encompassing ways to resolve or satisfy other interests: some psychological ones, like self-fulfillment, prestige, recognition, sense of belonging; other non-monetary ones such as security, guarantees, precedent, delivery options, etc.

In addition, the Child ego state provides intuition and emotions and will perceive emotions from the other side as well as their subtle nonverbal messages. Their emotions, intuitive understanding and grasping of nonverbal messages in the course of negotiations are true subjective indicators of how things are going, signs that the adult must process and combine rationally to attain the best outcomes. The Child is responsible for creating empathy, good vibes and rapport, and whenever the adult assessment deems it convenient, the Child will bring in humor and relaxation facilitating a congenial and relaxing working relationship.

What if Someone Plays Out of Tune?

Problems often arise in negotiations when inappropriately using an ego state under certain circumstances or when undergoing a specific moment.

A similar situation occurs with a percussion player in an orchestra, he falls asleep and when suddenly awakens, he bangs hard on the drums at the exact moment the flute was to play a solo.

It is not advisable to use the Parent ego state when building creative options (beyond its role in laying the rules for brainstorming.)

Neither is it advisable to use the Child ego state when examining the appropriateness of legitimacy, standards and market value criteria.

Using the Adult ego state to set a humorous tone, attain relaxation or create empathy and good vibes in a working relationship is typically not the best choice.

General framing for the negotiation	Parent: Suggests rules on how we will negotiate. Adult: Suggests the agenda for an efficient process. Child: Creates good vibes, empathy and rapport.	
NEGOTIATION ELEMENT	EGO STATE	CONTRIBUTES
Interests. Needs, concerns, motives, hopes that encourage us to negotiate.	Child	The nuts and bolts of negotiation: desires, yearnings, tastes, fears, worries, et cetera.
	Adult	Turns positions into interests and develops goals and objectives.
Options. Reasonable possibilities to reach an agreement with the people you are negotiating with - at the negotiation table.	Parent	Permission to think and safeguarding rules to avoid early criticism. Then, criticizes based on values and legitimacy standards.
	Adult	Evaluates ideas, filters, examines realism, applies rational methods for decision-making, and separates the invention process from decision-making.
	Child	Creativity, curiosity, intuition and inventiveness to create new ideas.
Alternative. What you can do for yourself and others without agreement from the opposite side to satisfy your interests – away from the table.	Parent	Permission to think and rules to avoid early criticism.
	Adult	Assessment of alternatives versus interest-based options for decision-making.
	Child	Creativity, curiosity, intuition and inventiveness.
Legitimacy. All persuasion obtained based on accepted rules and objective standards and criteria.	Parent	Custom, usage, decrees, rules, standards.
	Adult	Updates information. Creates new standards.
Commitment. Oral or written declarations on what parties will or will not do.	Adult	Realism, operational capacity, functionality.
Communication. Verbal or nonverbal message exchange.	Adult	Inquires into and presents data. Ensures understanding and being understood. Questions Parent assumptions and prejudices.

Working relationship. Parties' skills to effectively and assertively manage their differences.	Parent	Emotions and values such as trust and credibility.
	Adult	Separates substance from relationship.
	Child	Emotions, empathy, sense of humor, good vibes and relaxation.

What if Any of the Three Sings Out of Tune or Doesn't Know How to Play?

Most likely your Child has already discovered that Berne's division into Parent, Adult and Child ego states is extremely useful and, at times, enough to better understand why our negotiations are successful or have failed.

All the so-called pathologies of the ego have an impact on how we negotiate and the results attained.

Next we will examine some of the typical and representative «out of tune» players as well as their impact on negotiations to help understand the concept and provide us with a practical tool for self-diagnosis and diagnosing those with whom we negotiate.

Exclusions

Exclusion is that situation where an individual's use of one of the ego states is so constant and intense that it invalidates or practically renders the other two and their functions inexistent.

Excluding Parent

Some people present an overly developed Parent ego state which poses an imbalance. An archetype of this group could be a preacher or religious or political fanatic. We are all aware of the consequences when a group, community or a nation is led by this type of individual, as well as the kinds of conflicts or negotiations involved.

They tend to act dogmatically, hardly flexible, full of prejudices and past preconceptions often obsolete, which they mix up with objective and updated legitimacy criteria.

Typically included in their conversations are "you must", "you mustn't", "you should", "you shouldn't'", "you can", "you can't", etc. (modal operators of necessity and possibility.)

In certain cases, the nature of the work or profession fosters over development of this ego state in some negotiators.

For example: Some lawyers or members of insurance companies whose work boils down to complying with legislation or what is written in procedural handbooks (what should be done) reflect this trend in the type of commitments reached.

The relationship is embodied by "I'm OK, you are not OK", with very little chance of relaxation or sense of humor, poor dealing with emotions and intuition and strong use of hierarchical order.

Often acting critically, lecturing and preaching; at other times being paternalistic and overprotective ("do as I say", "I know what's good for you") involving a one-way communication mode.

As a result of the amount of limiting beliefs there is little room for mistakes thus fewer opportunities to encourage a creative environment for enabling multiple value-added options or out-of-the-box thinking or ideas, all of which weaken negotiation results.

Excluding Adult

At other times, the Adult ego state is overdeveloped creating an imbalance at the expense of the other two ego states.

A prototype of this group could be an engineer, a physicist or dehumanized mathematician, or Mr. Spock from *Star Trek*.

Negotiators in this group are cold, hyper rational and create scarcely empathetic working relationships and communication, lacking rapport, sense of humor and relaxation; becoming robotic in extreme cases.

They lack skills to understand and deal with "human" interests (fears, concerns, wishes, etc.) or to acknowledge and deal with their own and others' emotions.

Oftentimes geared toward achievements –typically not enjoyed–, seeking results, effectiveness and efficiency; what is most convenient without considering what parties wish, and in some cases, not even considering what should be done.

As is to be expected, these negotiators are weak in creativity skills. In contrast, they are good in managing the agenda and process, as well as in quantitative decision-making, the use of objective mathematical criteria and rational methods that minimize uncertainty, intuition or any other human interference.

Excluding Child

Finally, negotiators with this egogram are typically represented by artists in different disciplines and ad agency creatives.

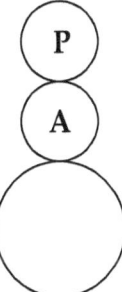

These negotiators are often emotional, impulsive, chaotic, who come to negotiations with little to no preparation.

Their thinking is magical and their ideas are often superstitious or tend to follow "hunches".

They dislike agendas and order in the process, and in extreme situations they may turn a negotiation chaotic.

When faced with difficulties they typically adopt a positional attitude, sometimes whimsical or yearning, labile, fickle; at times unruly, at times yielding, sometimes elated and others depressed.

They are manipulative mixing substance with relationship, occasionally from a victim stance, seeking to make others feel guilty, threatening to break up the relationship if not given what is requested or through emotional blackmailing.

Decision-making is impulsive, unpredictable, not very rational or logical and without measuring results.

Consequently, they may reach voluntaristic agreements, barely realistic, sometimes hard to live up to or inconvenient or unattainable, even when objectively they would be absolutely convenient.

It is unlikely for them to consider what to do in case the negotiation fails (alternatives) and many times, when faced with the idea, they discredit and accuse the opposing party of undermining their spirit.

Legitimacy criteria, standards and rules are not exactly the tools they best handle or welcome readily; on the contrary, they typically go against them.

Creativity is their strength though at times they require some help to be efficient and practical.

A special note for work teams

When we negotiate individually, any of the above described personality pathologies could impact negatively on negotiation results.

When we negotiate in teams, some pathologies may be tuned down and occasionally turned into advantages.

Many work groups comprise people who tend to overuse some of the ego states to the detriment of the others; yet in different combinations and proportions we can integrate negotiating teams where complementarity boosts results.

If we are somehow able to manage individuals at the timeliest moment during preparation, negotiation and evaluation —for example, more of a Child ego state at the time of creating ideas, more of an Adult ego state to later assess these ideas and avoid anticipated criticism from those who have an overly developed Parent ego state—, we could tap into our differences and change what could be a threat to results obtained into an advantage in our negotiations.

Contamination

This occurs in cases where information contained in the Adult ego state of an individual is partly mixed with information stemming from Parent (prejudiced ideas) and Child (magical or superstitious thought) ego states.

Opinions of these people sound adult, i.e. calm, safe and unhurried thus sometimes they and other people they negotiate with believe so. Nevertheless, if carefully examined they do not have a rational foundation and are upheld with pseudo-scientific arguments.

Not too long ago, in the course of a workshop two participants got into a discussion.

One of them, a therapist, posited that around 60% of all emergency consultations in general hospitals were situations where there was a psychosomatic element to the emergency.

There was also a doctor in the group who quickly rejected that statement and so a pseudo-scientific dialogue ensued between two contaminated adults.

The therapist pseudo-demonstrated that her assertion was correct, *because she had read it,* though she could not recall exactly the source.

The doctor pseudo-demonstrated it was not so because he worked in the emergency setting and *according to his own personal experience* such was not the case.

A Parent who relies on non-reliable sources (what is written is true) and a Child poorly using the inductive method (draws a universal rule from just a few cases), would have had a similar discussion.

PARENT CONTAMINATION	CHILD CONTAMINATION	DOUBLE CONTAMINATION
"Never trust women, and worse still when negotiating."	*"I can't find my good-luck tie. I'd better cancel the negotiation."*	*"Oh boy, what a bummer! Today I get to negotiate with two women."*

So What's Worse?

This is a fairly common question in our courses and consulting work, and the right answer would be "Worse than what, specifically?", or perhaps the most typical of all consultants' answers is: "It depends."

However, if we consider the question refers to which of the problems mentioned impacts more on negotiation results, I would say that when people make decisions –and that is what negotiations are about–:

♦ If made from the Parent ego state, these take into account a great number of limitations, prejudices, preconceptions as well as legitimacy criteria. The Parent is protective, uses self-critique, criticizes the others and proposals presented at the table, thus risks of making a really wrong decision are not so high.

♦ The same holds true when parties operate with a high Adult ego state during negotiations. Like in the previous case, creativity and empathy may be utterly lacking yet decisions will most certainly be weighed and, where possible, measured and compared often before they are made.

♦ Experience shows that when a person prepares, negotiates and evaluates results from the Child ego state the situation is riskier. By no means ruling out the value of intuition, typically exalted in these instances, when we find ourselves "possessed by our magical spirit" and against any reasoning consider ourselves defeated or invincible, decision-making could be catastrophic. When a manager is delighted and thinks "Today nothing can go wrong because it's the 13th," or depressed because "I lost my good-luck pencil holder," it is advisable to negotiate some time to think, get advice and resume a more assertive method to negotiate and decide.

Some of those dialogues may be positive for the individual; for example, when our internal Parent encourages us to overcome some difficulty ("Go on, you're doing great!")

Is It a Matter of Negotiating Internally?

Internal dialogues

Sometimes problems in negotiations are related to existing internal dialogues.

These communications take place between Parent-Child without the Adult being aware of it.

This occurs as circuits that repeat themselves several times a day, at times they externalize, like when we see people on the street talking to themselves, often involved in inner conversations which they are unaware of.

At other times those dialogues scare, anger and depress us or even make us reply inappropriately, just like at some point in our lives one of our external parental figures did, or as did occur during the negotiation I commented on earlier in this chapter. It is possible I acted then in response to an unconscious internal dialogue where my fight-picking parental side (P), devoid of my Adult analysis, said to my Child:

P: "Julio, that's downright abusive, you saw that house with the mural and all and now they want to take it away from you; you deserve some respect, don't give in." (1)

C: "You're right, should I tell him off?" (2)

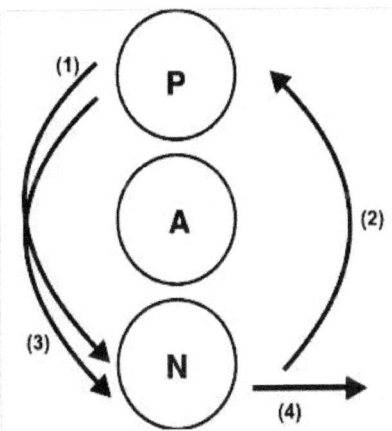

Results of these internal dialogues on negotiations depend on the type of dialogue, but if they are in any way similar to my story —and we don't have a friend at hand— they could be catastrophic.

Congruence and incongruence

In creating what we later came to know as personality functional analysis, Berne used five observable behavioral cues: body posture, gestures, facial expression, tone of voice and type of language used.

This list was expanded to twelve cues by Doctor Roberto Kertesz et al.

THE TWELVE CUES OF OBJECTIVE (EXTERNAL, PUBLIC) BEHAVIOR	
CUES OF VERBAL BEHAVIOR (LANGUAGE)	1. Words and phrases; syntax. 2. Tones of voice. 3. Speech rhythm, speed. 4. Volume (intensity.)
NON VERBAL BEHAVIOR (BODILY)	5. Gaze (pupil expression.) 6. Facial expression (facial muscles.) 7. Gestures and mannerisms (hands, arms, legs, feet, neck, shoulders, head movements.) 8. Body posture (trunk, hips.) 9. Vegetative elements (skin color, muscle tone, sweat, heart beats, breathing rhythm, lower lip volume.) 10. Physical distance vis-à-vis others. 11. Pace and speed of body movements. 12. Garments (clothing, accessories, make-up.)

Each one of these cues conveys a message which can be congruent or incongruent with the rest.

We say there is congruence when all of an individual's behavioral cues (ours or the counterparties') convey the same message.

There is incongruence when different behavioral cues convey distinct messages.

Incongruence can be simultaneous or sequential.

In simultaneous incongruence some behavioral cues convey different messages at the same time. Thus these types of incongruences may often go unnoticed to the counterparty's conscious mind triggering a funny response and more often confusion.

Example: A negotiator says, *"Let's examine this calmly, please!"* while

yelling and pounding on the table.

Example: The leader of a brainstorming session for a negotiation group preparation says: *"We will start the session and please remember we shouldn't criticize ideas, we are just inventing,"* and minutes later, when someone comes up with a different idea, jumps up and says: *"That's so stupid, it's ridiculous, they would never accept that kind of thing."*

Unless intended, that is, decided by the Adult ego state for a specific purpose (to annoy, confuse, etc.), any of these situations (as in the case of internal dialogues) deserve a true internal, intrapersonal negotiation prior to the external and interpersonal one due to potential negative consequences.

If that is the case, we suggest agreeing with your own players, first on who should play, then the sequencing and the how; in doing so, the "empty chair" procedure proves to be best. It will be described at the end of the chapter.

The Orchestra Expands: Functional Analysis of Ego States

Based on our recordings and subsequent analysis of these observable behavioral cues —as found often in our advanced workshops and personal consulting work—, it is possible to define the following ego state subdivisions:

The Parent is subdivided into:

CP (CRITICAL PARENT)
Positive side: firm behavior, order, control, setting appropriate limits.
Negative side: prejudices, insults, belittling, authoritarian.

NP (NURTURING OR PROTECTIVE PARENT)
Supports others' growth, protection, understanding, permission to live, enjoy and grow, education and orientation. *Negative side:* overprotective.

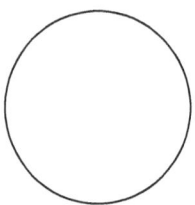

FREE CHILD (FC)
includes a biological part: NC or NATURAL CHILD and AC or ADULT CHILD (intuition, creativity, curiosity, liveliness.) Not differentiated by objective behavioral cues.

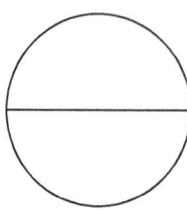

The Adult ego state is not functionally subdivided since you cannot allocate distinct behavioral cues to supposed divisions.

We have, however, classified them into three levels:
Lowest: *muscular.* It executes mechanical tasks with muscles.
Intermediate: *Repetitive intellectual.* Only fulfills intellectual tasks told by others (spreadsheets, etc.)
Highest: *analytical.* Studies data from reality, self-programming, plans. These levels are important when analyzing employment tasks, staff selection and training.

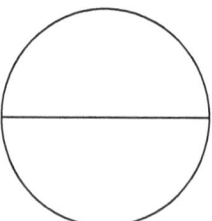

How do we realize what part of the Parent ego state works? **Internally**, through our thoughts and feelings. **Externally**, when hearing our voice recorded, watching ourselves in a videotape or mirror and observing others through behavioral cues (words, tones of voice, gestures, etc.)

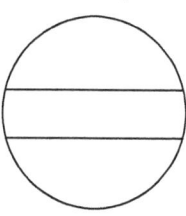

THE ADAPTED CHILD (AC)
Originates in the FREE CHILD gradually adapting to family and environmental demands. Comprises two sub-ego states: the SUBMISSIVE/ COMPLIANT CHILD (obedient, disciplined, sometimes belittled), and the REBELLIOUS CHILD (opposing, defiant, provoking, competitive.)

Structure recommended for daily practice purposes

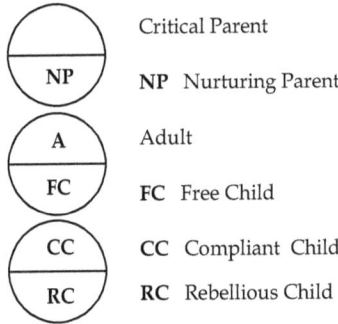

Critical Parent

NP Nurturing Parent

Adult

FC Free Child

CC Compliant Child

RC Rebellious Child

Some Further "Instruments"

In addition, this instrument enables the fine-tuning of distinctions in a practical and simple way, available to any interested observer.

Where applicable, we can differentiate positive and negative sides of the ego states thus enlarging the orchestra to twelve members.

POSITIVE AND NEGATIVE BEHAVIORAL SYSTEM

NEGATIVE SYSTEM (NOT - OK)	POSITIVE SYSTEM (OK)
Authoritarian aggressor, prejudiced.	Firm, serious, fair, correct, organizer.
Overprotective, mushy. Prevents others from growing.	Affectionate, nurturing, warm. Let's live and enjoy.
Not informed or poorly informed. Robotic-like (hard-wired by the NOT – OK Parent or by the adapted NOT – OK Child) Dishonest, calculating. **A-**	**A** Ethical, informed, responsible.
Selfish, cruel, brutal, rude. Manipulative.	Lively, affectionate, wants enjoyment, feels authentic emotions. Creative, curious, intuitive.
Belittled, fearful, anxious.	Disciplined.
Aggressive, rancorous, challenging.	Rejects, injustices and skewed views.

Our Goal: Help Create Options

Many melodies are possible with 12 musicians.

Repeatedly, poor results in negotiations arise from using obsolete styles that prove inappropriate for the situation and lack flexibility where negotiators strictly use just a few and inadequate ego states.

SOFT IN EVERYTHING	HARD IN EVERYTHING
• "We must talk." • I insist on preserving the friendship. • I start off with a reasonable position. • I make concessions to build the relationship. • I make an offer.	• "We don't have to talk." • I insist on my position. • I begin with an extreme position. • I demand concessions as a condition to maintain the relationship. • I threaten.
Ego states used automatically and repetitively.	Ego states used automatically and repetitively.
Inadequate nurturing Parent. Inadequate compliant Child.	Inadequate critical Parent. Inadequate rebellious Child.

The most relevant general goal of this chapter is to open up possibilities for a greater number of options to answers vis-à-vis different stimuli in the course of our negotiations.

Overall in life, and particularly in negotiations, one of the secrets to success is flexibility; that is, having the capacity and resources to expand the repertoire of ways to satisfy our interests.

Although as a rule we discourage the use of inadequate forms, all ego states, data and programs stored therein during our lifetime are options and resources readily available to answer to reality's demands.

Knowing and arranging them during our negotiations, like surgeons arrange their instrumentation, enable us to use them at the right time, in the right way, and in the appropriate sequence to achieve our goals most efficiently and elegantly.

Our Recommendation: First Diagnose, Then Answer

One of the general recommendations which is greatly universal in negotiations is: *first diagnose, then answer as you consider most conveniently.*

This recommendation aims to avoid one of the most common errors: reacting rather than acting proactively.

The difference between both answers is the participation of the Adult ego state during the diagnostic period as well as the choice of the ego state from where it is most convenient to answer to a given situation.

Reacting to a situation is more related to an automatic response; without the Adult ego state participation one of the other ego states ties into the "invitation" by the other party.

In such cases we often forget our goals and real interests; we get involved in a different game where power is out of our realm and in the hands of those we react against.

In these occasions we suggest the following steps:

First step: Who is playing now?

The first step is to acknowledge and diagnose which of the other party's and my ego states are negotiating at a given time.

Eric Berne described four ways to recognize which ego state is in control for both you and your counterpart. This may be very easy when the person is using an ego state archetype and the four diagnostic tools can be used *and* they match.

However, other cases may be more complicated, especially if the four diagnostic elements do not match or, as during negotiations, we cannot access data from our counterpart.

Behavioral diagnosis: Behavioral diagnosis is based on observation of behavioral clues, especially words, tone of voice, facial expression, gestures and body postures.

EGO STATES	BEHAVIORAL CUES				
	Words	**Tone of voice**	**Facial expression**	**Gestures**	**Body postures**
CRITICAL PARENT	You should… You must… Shame.	Imperative. Critical. Mocking.	Frowning. Mouth corners downwards.	Finger-pointing. Arms crossed. Fists on hips. Jaw raised.	Straight back (haughty, arrogant.)
NURTURING PARENT	Poor thing… You are capable. You can count on me. Congratulations.	Pitiful. Affectionate. Warm. Cordial.	Smiley. Understanding. Mouth corners upwards.	Open arms. Arms embracing or leaning on head or shoulders.	Chest bent forward towards others.
ADULT	That's correct. Why? Data indicate that…	Uniform. Modulated.	Calm. Alert. Concentrated. Horizontal lips.	Hand holding chin (telephone position.) Forefinger upwards.	Straight posture, no tension, natural. Bent towards objects.
FREE CHILD	Aw! How nice! I like / dislike it. I want/I don't want.	Strong, tuneful. Innocent. Filled with emotion.	Shows emotions (rage, sadness, happiness, etc.) Fickle regarding emotions.	Uninhibited, spontaneous. Legs apart.	Free. Stretched out. Relaxed. On the floor.
SUBMISSIVE/ COMPLIANT CHILD	Please. I'll try. I don't know if I can. I should… I find it hard.	Mournful. Compliant. Tearful. Ups and downs.	Fearful (avoids looking straight into the eyes.) Downcast.	Covering up. Wringing hands. Shrugging shoulders. Overall tension.	Contracted. Stooped.
REBELLIOUS CHILD	I don't care. I don't feel like it. I'm coming. I'm coming… (never does).	Defying. Hostile.	Provocative, defying. Tight lower lip.	Tightened fists. Bragging. Stamping. Shrugging shoulders.	Sticking chest out, defying.

Social diagnosis: It is based on ego states of those surrounding a person in response to the latter's ego state. For example, when observing the ego states of a boss's collaborators during internal negotiations within the company we could diagnose which ego state the boss most likely displayed in those meetings.

In addition, if in the course of a negotiation I have a notion of my own ego state, it is likely that I will be able to infer that of my counterparty creating it.

Historical diagnosis: It is based on the memories of an individual triggered by the moment being experienced, like childhood scenes or copying other people's models into current behaviors.

Within the negotiation framework, this tool is only valid for intrapersonal diagnosis, since it is not advisable to ask the opposite side: "Do you recall any relative of yours being so stubborn and grouchy?"

Nevertheless, its value is far from negligible, particularly when considering what was said about social diagnosis; that is, when we know our own ego state we can then infer which of our counterparty's ego state is being invited.

Phenomenological diagnosis: It is based on what a person thinks and feels at a given time. During negotiations the same considerations as for the historical diagnosis hold true.

To help us diagnose and later respond in our negotiations, it will be extremely useful to know what we call "special invitations."

Each ego state one of the parties acts under at a given time specially invites one (or more) ego state/s of the counterpart to hook up to.

Thus if I am clear about the ego state under which I am acting I may predict what ego state from the opposite side I am inviting to answer.

Likewise, according to the ego state I hook up to as a result of something the other party said or did, I may diagnose under what ego state that individual is acting.

a) The Adult of one party often invites the Adult of the other.

> *Example:* A1 *"How about starting off the meeting by setting the purpose and end product?"*
> A2: *"Very well, how about the purpose being to present and respond to the interests of both parties and as end product an itemized list of those interests?"*

b) The Free Child of one of the parties often invites the Free Child of the other and occasionally the Controlling or Nurturing Parent.

> *Example:* FC1: *"Some coffee would be great right now!"*
> FC2: *"Yes, let's stop for a leg stretch."* How about getting some cookies too for that coffee?"
> CP: *"Come on, take things seriously. Now is not the time for coffee breaks; we're preparing a very important negotiation."*
> NP: *"Are you tired? It's only natural; you've been working hard on this case. Take a break while we tidy things up."*

b) The Submissive Child often invites the Nurturing or Critical Parent of the other side.

> Example: SC: *"I don't know. I never understand the difference between alternatives and options. I think negotiating is not for me."*
>
> CP: *"That's because you don't pay attention; you're always distracted."*
>
> NP: *"Allow me to explain. Alternatives and options are words often used synonymously, thus the confusion."*

c) The Rebellious Child of one of the parties often invites the Critical Parent of the other and occasionally the Rebellious Child.

> Example: RC: *"Truthfully, I'm a bit tired of you. You know there are other suppliers in the market; you're not the only ones, so…"*
> CP: *"That was a low blow. Threatening is not a good way of negotiating."*
>
> RC: *"And just so that you know: There are plenty of clients like you."*

d) The Critical Parent of one of the parties often invites the Submissive or Rebellious Child of the other party.

> Example: CP: *"You are pretty untidy with numbers and there are mistakes here. Not serious but in the end they are mistakes."*
>
> SC: *"I can't believe it. I got it wrong again?"*
>
> RC: *"Hey, if they're not so important, stop splitting hairs."*

e) Other times the Critical Parent of the other side is invited and both criticize a third party.

> Example: CP: *"Well, you know how public servants are these days. You can't trust them with anything, least of all with numbers."*

f) If the Nurturing Parent is appropriate, the NP will invite the Free Child of the other side.

> Example: NP: *"I see you've become emotional. I respect your feelings. What can I do for you?"*
> FC: *"Thank you. You've already helped me by just listening. I feel better."*

g) If inappropriate, the NP will often do so with the Submissive Child and, occasionally, with the Rebellious Child.

> Example: NP: *"Everything you know you owe to me. I helped you join the company and I taught you like a son. I believe you deserve recognition, and when I say you should accept the deal it's because I know what's best for you."*
>
> SC: *"Well, I don't know. Okay. If you say so."*
>
> RC: *"Who cares! You think you have a right to tell me what clothes to wear?" You're crazy."*

Bearing in mind these tools, especially when things are not going well, the first questions to posit from an Adult mode are:

Under what ego state am I operating?

Which is the ego state I perceive in the opposite side?

What is my counterpart saying or doing that hooks up with my ego state?

What am I saying or doing that may be hooking up with the other side's ego state?

Second step: changing the game (from reactive to proactive.)

One of the ways of handling our emotions during negotiations is acknowledging that you are becoming emotional and give the emotion a name. Equally effective is to be able to reflect enough to diagnose which ego states from both sides are negotiating; in doing so we will have taken great strides towards controlling the situation as an adult.

The following step is to determine if the ego states in control are appropriate; if the answer is no, which would be the most convenient ego state/s to undertake for that particular circumstance.

In this case we suggest asking the following questions:

From what ego state will my answer be more effective to achieve what I want?

What must I say or do differently to change the game?

Choose the answer you consider most appropriate from various possible ones and apply it.

Should you need to request time and leave the room for a few minutes to reflect and give your Adult control over the situation to achieve it, do so; that time will bring back invaluable benefits.

As a general guideline, in the following table we include some suggestions for choosing the ego state from which to respond, according to your diagnosis of the other party:

"Attack him where he is unprepared"

SunTzu

Sometimes, however, when facing this decision, you will recognize that several ego states fight from within to take control.

If you have diagnosed the other person to be	We suggest to use
Critical Parent (often hiding a fearful, resentful or sad Child)	Nurturing Parent when starting the exchange. Adult, assertively confronting. Free Child, articulating true emotion appropriately.
Inappropriate Nurturing Parent (intends to save us)	Adult separating the relationship from the substance.
Adult	Adult
Inappropriate Free Child (not taking anything seriously)	Adult, and if it doesn't work Critical Parent, setting limits.
Submissive Child (insecure)	Nurturing Parent to begin the exchange and then Adult.
Rebellious Child	Nurturing Parent looking for the hidden Free Child and pacing the emotion; and then Adult.

In these cases, and like in internal dialogues and incongruity, we suggest using the magic of meta-position with the "empty chair" procedure.

In fact you will need three empty chairs, one for each ego state.

Place them shaping a triangle and decide where you will seat each of your ego states.

The aim is to externalize, identify and reveal your inner parts, as well as differences of opinion in a safe setting and create dialogue between them.

Our most important recommendation is: when you find yourself seated in the chair bearing a specific ego state, act that part truly and speak in first person singular.

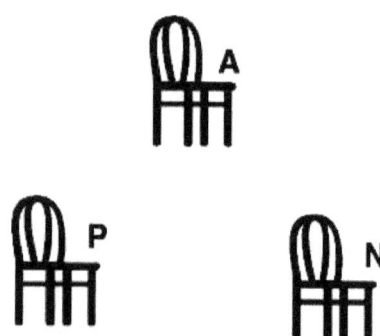

Develop dialogues rotating chairs as many times as considered convenient.

Negotiate internally the same way three (or more) people would in real life.

Thus you will be able to set limits between parties, create options, choose the best and reach internal agreements regarding which is the best intervention strategy of your ego states in each instance and under the Adult control.

Third step: Assess the results of your counterpart.

Once again using behavioral clues from the other negotiator, assess whether what you have done has reaped the expected results.

If so, go ahead; otherwise, our general recommendation is: *if something did not work out, try something else.*

You now have a good repertoire of possibilities to attain it.

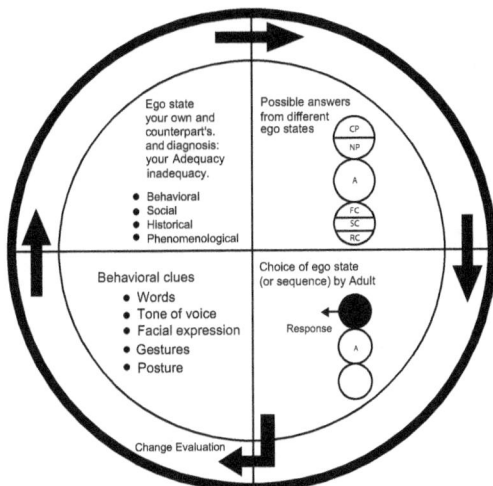

Practice, Practice, Practice

Once, while visiting the city of an important museum dedicated to all worldwide famous athletes, a tourist asked a local person: "How do I get to the athletes' Hall of Fame?"

The villager looked him up and down slowly and replied: "Practice, practice, practice."

Just like people who learn how to ride a bike or drive a car, you can change your inappropriate automatic behaviors, going through a period where you will have to think and take your time to consciously resolve.

During that time you will probably have to think which masks and disguises to use, and *when* something appears to be mechanical, making you feel uncomfortable, and even funny or somewhat eccentric at times.

However, like in any other learning process, after that period you will almost certainly start a period of unconscious competence, that is, with no need to pay special attention; your Adult ego state will diagnose and adequately and automatically resolve the majority of difficult situations that arise.

If practiced during your negotiations, you will soon notice yourself using it to your benefit in other areas in life, as an added value, thus contributing not only to improve results thereof but also to your personal growth.

For That Difficult Negotiation Coming Up Next:

My Parent ego state says: *Go ahead, you can do it!*

My Adult says to you: *Prepare yourself well using all the tools in the book.*

My Child says to you: *I wish you great success from the bottom of my heart.*

CHAPTER 6

How to Resolve Conflicts: Like Bambi or Like Rambo?

Why Learn Principled Negotiation?

The Usual Way of Resolving Conflicts

A quick insight illustrates how each individual is able to have an overall idea of how he or she usually solves conflicts and disputes involved in whether social, work or family-related or any other kind of conflicts.

When saying a 'usual' way reference is made to a trend, and it means not always or not necessarily in all cases things are done that way. However, a prevalent pattern, way or style of behavior, thoughts, feelings and emotions could certainly be recognized.

Likewise, individuals probably also perform a self-evaluation or grade themselves on whether problem-solving is appropriate or inappropriate and whether they are skilled or not in that field. Often, but not always, this assessment stems from a poorly objective perception of feelings and emotions experienced before, during and after the conflict.

In other cases, it is the result of external opinions and the value attributed to them.

In any case, both factors can be combined in varying degrees in different people. If grading is done in this way, it will also be well funneled and influenced by the general opinion or value individuals have of themselves (self-esteem) and beliefs related to their own ability and that of others on the subject.

The goals of this chapter and the following exercise are as follows:

1. To help perceive typical behavioral modes when confronted with conflicts.

2. To establish the possible source of each one's style and different classic problem-solving styles.

3. To suggest a different way of evaluating behaviors and a road towards change, if the latter is intended.

Exercise

After reading the instructions to the following exercise, where possible, look for a quiet and calm place, sit comfortably, relax your body and close your eyes for a few minutes: everything will feel easier and clearer.

Even if you are unable to do it under these circumstances, just by reading it you will notice enough to answer the following questions.

I am walking around a supermarket and I notice a familiar face amongst the crowd. I realize this is a person I'm in conflict with, someone with whom issues are pending.

As the person approaches, several possibilities cross my mind on what to do and how to handle the situation, and I choose one.

That moment is over.

What possibilities went through your mind?

Which did you finally choose?

How do you feel or felt with that choice?

What is the connection between this response and your usual conflict or problem-solving way and your ulterior feelings?

Generically speaking, the following are behavioral probabilities when facing conflict:

1. Avoidance.

2. Postponement or delay.

3. Facing or coping.

Numbers 1 and 3 basically relate to human conventional and inherited responses when faced with a stressful agent or element.

When confronted with a threat, the prehistoric human being, like the current one, was physiologically prepared for flight (escape) or fight (until the threat was removed or else death.)

Unlike thousands of years ago the current civilization imposes on the human being the impossibility (real or imaginary) of flight and of exercising the trend to destroy the tension-producing object. Meanwhile, conflict modes multiply.

Every day at the workplace, on the street, in the family setting and in social activities situations appear where inner needs clash against the needs of others. If we also include internal dialogues (intrapersonal) where ideas and feelings sometimes endlessly clash, it is obvious, even in the absence of external stimuli, that you become a victim of conflict. Need and convenience force you to find new ways of resolving disputes; otherwise, the price is too high. Many psychosomatic diseases, even death, may be the final outcome.

Hence the ability to adequately resolve conflicts (the sum of a set of requirements) becomes very relevant. However, despite its importance, even the adult human being has the same tools —just a little more refined—as those learned during childhood to solve differences.

If the subject is not properly addressed, and data and training are lacking, the same obsolete programs will be repeated once and again, achieving scarce results that are justified by poorly arguing "that's just the way I am."

Avoiding / Postponing / Facing

Any of the listed possibilities (avoiding, postponing or facing) are not in and of themselves good or bad if used as part of a strategy and there is flexibility to change or combine them.

Avoiding, under certain circumstances, may be convenient and appropriate, yet if it becomes the usual way of conflict resolution it is almost certain that results attained will be objectively (if such term can be used in human matters) bad and resulting in poor personal satisfaction.

Postponing deserves similar considerations because it is a close relative of avoidance. When it becomes a habit it will not be problem-solving and no degree of satisfaction will be obtained.

At first sight *facing* seems to be the best possibility, provided that flexibility is maintained to strategically combine that option with previous ones, where applicable.

There are two ways of facing conflict: Using manipulation in its various forms: power, bribery, blame; and using negotiation skills.

Manipulating is using some basically dishonest behavior or conduct in pursuit of what a person wants from the other without asking or giving anything in exchange.

You learn how to use manipulative mechanisms since childhood from adults who, in turn, learned them from their elders. Depending on the "educating" role taken by parents or tutors (persecutor, victim, rescuer or a combination of both) will be the manipulative mechanism used in each case (fear, blame, and bribe.)

Persecutors manipulate through feelings of fear.

Victims manipulate through blame, making others feel guilty.

Rescuers (overprotective) manipulate through bribery.

To attain their goals all of them use the so-called exchange goods: Time, affection, recognition, data, material goods and services. Manipulation takes place either giving or taking away (administering) any of them.

In Table 6-1 there are some typical phrases of each manipulation type relative to each exchange good. The reader will recognize them as usual (some more than others) during his or her infancy and possibly in his or her current life.

Manipulative mechanism / Exchange goods	FEAR	BLAME	BRIBERY
TIME	If you misbehave, I'll leave.	You're doing this to me! I devoted my life to you!	If you behave well, I'll stay.
AFFECTION RECOGNITION	If you misbehave, I'll stop loving you.	I always loved you so much!	If you behave well, I will love you very much.
INFORMATION	If you misbehave, I won't tell you a story.	I always told you everything!	If you behave well, I'll tell you a story.
MATERIAL GOODS AND SERVICES	If you misbehave, I won't bring you candy.	I've always given you everything I had and more!	If you behave well, I'll bring you candy.

Table 6-1 Manipulation mechanisms

These manipulative mechanisms take on a different shape in adult life; sometimes more subtle that those appearing in the table above since in negotiations bribery is not as usual and concrete as when offering candy. At other times, it is much more daring. A person or nation threatens to use force (or uses it) if not given what asked for.

In the following exercise, an approach to real-life situations, check the corresponding box in the grid for the example vignettes listed below.

General context: A young executive finds out his salary is lower than other employees' who joined the company after him and serve in similar hierarchical positions, so he decides to ask for a raise. Upon requesting the wage increase, the manager and company owner answered:

♦ "You're asking me for a $ 5,000 raise now?

You're saying, pay me or I'm leaving, I've grown, and I don't need you anymore?

Is this how you repay me for my efforts, everything I've done for you?

You're doing this to me, I who was a father to you and taught you everything I know?

I really feel awful; you should be more considerate and acknowledge how much you've learnt from my advice. The truth is I'm devastated."

♦ "So you want to talk about money!

Okay. I talk about money all the time and if that's the ground you want to tread on, let's see. We'll become traders and argue over dollars and cents and if friendship or the future is damaged along the way, let it be so. Don't tell me later I didn't warn you; if we start this negotiation, other things will open up too."

♦ "Oh, boy!

You're asking for a raise just when we're about to open a new branch and wondering who of the company's promising young staff would be the right one to manage it. I don't know, think about it."

Manipulative mechanism / Exchange goods	FEAR	BLAME	BRIBERY
TIME			
AFFECTION RECOGNITION			
INFORMATION			
MATERIAL GOODS AND SERVICES			

Lastly, in the course of typical conflicts or disputes whether in organizations, communities, families or between individuals, the three modes are present in varying degrees. If you pay attention, its overall use is evident once and again since the most salient feature is repetition, hence involving very little creativity.

Alternatively, another way of facing conflicts is through negotiation, a procedure enabling adult and creative dispute resolution; generally, if carried out appropriately the results are more satisfactory for all parties involved.

Which Is Your Style?

When reference is made to appropriate or inappropriate negotiation it means the difference between assertive and principled negotiation, and conventional negotiator styles, soft or hard; generally it is a concealed version of "fight or flight" referred to here as "Rambo" or "Bambi" styles, respectively.

A SOFT NEGOTIATOR: "BAMBI"	A HARD NEGOTIATOR: "RAMBO"
Participants are friends.	Participants are adversaries.
The goal is agreement.	The goal is victory.
Make concessions to cultivate the relationship.	Demand concessions as a condition of the relationship.
Soft on the people and the problem.	Hard on the problem and the people.
Trust others.	Distrust others.
Change your position easily.	Dig in to your position.
Make offers.	Make threats.
Disclose your bottom line.	Mislead as to your bottom line.
Accept one-sided losses to reach agreement.	Demand one-sided gains as the price of agreement.
Search for the single answer: the one they will accept.	Search for the single answer: the one you will accept.
Insist on agreement.	Insist on your position.
Try to avoid a contest of wills.	Try to win a contest of wills.
Yield to pressure.	Apply pressure.

Table 6-3 Negotiation styles
Roger Fisher and William Ury. *Getting to yes: Negotiating Agreement Without Giving In, Houghton Mifilin Co.* Boston.
1981.

Negotiating Styles and Existential Position

Often the style reflects a basic position towards the world; it is intimately related to an existential position. Though the name sounds striking, the concept is simple.

Existential position is the way in which a person perceives him or herself relative to others, whether in terms of thoughts, images or feelings. In short, a notion of each one's regard for ownself and others, similar to what is known as self-esteem.

Based on how you have been "hardwired" by your parents, tutors, teachers, siblings, etc., a person may think of him or herself (sometimes consciously others not) as worthless, incapable or stupid, unlucky or unsuccessful and must try to gain the liking of others.

This position called "devalued" position is certainly the one adopted by a great majority of people, and it openly exposes a low self-esteem: I am not OK - you are OK (- +). Often the negotiating style is soft and the basic philosophy —as well as negotiation results— is "lose - win."

Conversely, a person may think of him or herself as very capable, intelligent, successful, deserving of respect and recognition by others whom he or she considers inferior or least gifted: "I am OK - You are not OK (+ -)." They feel they never make mistakes and if something goes wrong they are not responsible, they blame it on the one who failed to do what had to be done. This position is called "persecuting" position, the opposite of the devalued position.

In these cases, low self-esteem is concealed under a facade of power and toughness, behind a shield that is hard to endure and results in equal suffering than the former. Oftentimes the typically "hard" style (given an important drawback or failure) may reveal opposite and devaluing behavior, where called for. The basic philosophy when faced with conflict —and results pursued in negotiations— is "win-win"; yet if both negotiators display the same position disputes may end up being "lose-lose" or "who loses less."

The intensity of these unrealistic positions varies from slight —apparent only in extreme situations— to archetypal characters whom at the first available chance and almost always reveal their existential position traits.

Though in truth being two sides of the same coin, these two negotiating styles and existential positions may socially be perceived differently.

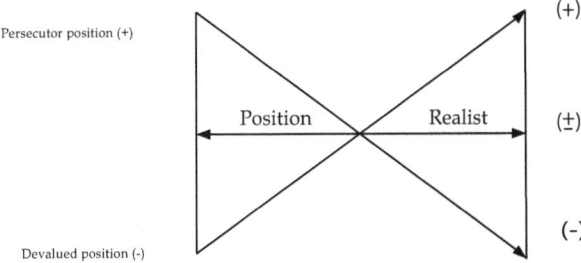

Figure 6-1 Existential position

A "Bambi" style can occasionally be perceived as conciliatory and seeking consensus, especially if all those involved display similar behaviors. Experience shows this negotiation style leads to poor outcomes resulting in fair and feasible agreements yet inefficient, leaving "money on the table", (that is, not attaining as much as possible) and of little personal satisfaction (as often the case when low self-esteem is openly articulated.)

Agreements are quickly reached but closed before thoroughly exploring all interests or creating enough value added options; or examining legitimacy criteria to weigh the fairness of options; or even without considering what parties could do to satisfy their interests, alone or with others, but away from the negotiation table.

A "Rambo" style is sometimes socially confused with a winner, especially when negotiating with a "Bambi" style person. However, when considering medium and long-term results, opinions may change, particularly when there remains a group of people with feelings of rancor, remorse, revenge and resentment (the four 'Rs' of the Apocalypse) who will transform the wounded "Bambis" into silent saboteurs or hard opponents ("Rambos") whenever they get a chance.

Beyond these feelings, the person "negotiating" from this position frequently feels unsatisfied thinking he or she "could have gotten more" or that "despite it all, he or she may have been misled" or "he deserved more."

Triumphalism (or false triumph) is not the same as being triumphant. The angst of potentially losing (real or imaginary) is coupled with sleeplessness, ulcers, infarction or an unsatisfactory family life, not to mention the reaction someone bearing this style might have given an "ill-deserved defeat" at the hands of those "never considered equal."

The *Pareto Principle* enables a graphic and clear representation of the results of different negotiating style combinations (See Figure 6-2.)

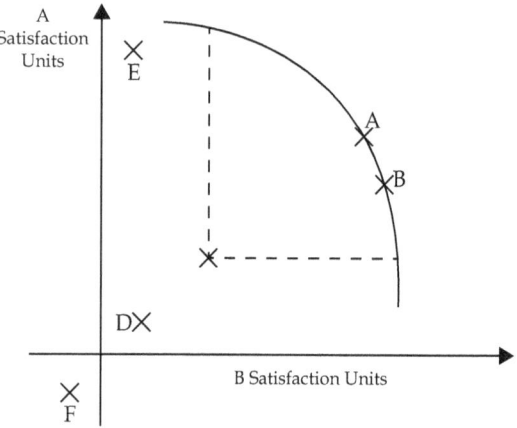

Figure 6-2 The Pareto Principle

Pareto, the great Italian economist, stated that in a world with limited, finite resources there comes a point in any negotiation where agreement between parties achieves the maximum efficiency level, measured in degrees of satisfaction of both parties' needs or interests (point A.) Therefore, to continue negotiating would be in the domain of a "zero sum game", i.e. one of the party's gain (if the party wanted more) equals the other party's loss (point B.)

Any other agreement reached within the boundary (point C) could be improved by either party without being detrimental to the other, or, the opposite, may also achieve additional benefits.

Considering the traits of this style, experience shows that when "Bambis" negotiate agreements these are often doable and fair yet unproductive for both sides (point D.)

When a "Rambo" and a "Bambi" negotiate agreements often could still be feasible but they are generally unfair and efficient for a short term, and only for one of the parties, of course the "Rambo" style party (point E.)

When two "Rambos" negotiate it is possible that no agreement be reached even if there are one or several convenient options for both. The measure of success in such cases is often established by who won more or less than the other (point F.) This measurement system reminds us more of the way in which war results are measured rather than negotiations: how many overall casualties and how many were the enemy's. In these negotiations, like in armed conflicts, it is pointless to talk about who won since it depends on who you are comparing yourself with.

Lastly, a realistic existential position "I'm OK - You're OK" (+/-+/-) means that one individual acknowledges his or her own defects and weaknesses without feeling belittled, as well as own virtues and strengths without feeling superior. Likewise, it means to be able to acknowledge that others, too, have virtues and weaknesses without having to worship or degrade them.

This is the only position that relates to good self-esteem and personal assurance and the one that mostly improves the possibility of developing an assertive, principled negotiation style, based on a "win-win" philosophy. Within the assertive style, participants do joint problem-solving as their goal is to achieve a sensible result efficiently and amicably.

Principled Negotiation

Negotiating with an assertive, principle-based style —neither hard nor soft — (typical of a realistic position) means to follow some basic rules, tenets or propositions that act as general behavioral guidelines in all negotiations you are involved in.

Principled negotiation refers to using the following ideas and general recommendations as groundwork for your actions:

♦ Separate the people from the problem: solve the "soft-hard" dilemma by treating people gently and being hard on substantive issues. Do not forget that "courtesy costs nothing but gains everything." Do not confuse people's opinions with their value as human beings. It is not advisable to trust naïvely, yet even in those circumstances where it is best not to trust, better be reliable and treat both aspects separately.

♦ Focus on interests, not positions: Find out what lies behind what people say about what they want or need. Inquire why or what they need it for; explore their real needs, what they truly want to achieve, their wishes, desires, as well as fears, concerns and what they are afraid of losing. Avoid adopting an extreme position that will not allow opening options to reach a solution.

♦ Invent options for mutual gain: Separate the process of inventing and creating ideas from the process of deciding. Develop multiple possible solutions; look for creative ways (material and non-material) to add value; try to approach the limits of Pareto's principle. Then decide by combining the ideas that contribute more to parties' interests.

♦ Insist on using objective criteria: Look for results based on legitimate standards, objective criteria alien to the will or whim of the parties. Think through and be open to reasoning on these grounds. Do not let yourself be manipulated or coerced yet keep permeable to what is fair and objective; this grants more power of persuasion.

Based on the above, assessing your negotiating skills means not only considering emotions, feelings or external opinions (often distorted by the lens of a non-realistic existential position) but also examining results of each negotiation according to the model of what a good result should be.

Negotiation: A Good Result

A good result is when an agreement is reached that:

♦ Is better than your BATNA (Best Alternative to a Negotiated Agreement.)

♦ Satisfies interests: ours, well; theirs, well or at least acceptably; third parties', tolerably.

♦ Is a good solution: does not leave any waste; it is the best among many *options.*

♦ It is *legitimate* for everyone, where no one party has taken advantage of the other.

♦ It includes well-planned, realistic, operational and functional *commitments.*

♦ Shows that the process is efficient because there is good *communication.*

♦ Helps establish or strengthen the desired *working relationship.*

Why Is Principled Negotiation Convenient?

Learning to negotiate based on principles and adopting a realistic and assertive model is beneficial because:

♦ It helps improve conflict outcomes and personal satisfaction with such results.

♦ It aids in correcting the existential position (self-esteem and how you view others), which enables remaining "realistic" for a longer period. Although the opposite is also true, the mechanism through which this change operates is based on a principle stemming from behavioral psychology schools: "If you change what you say and do you will change what you think and feel." Human beings are equipped with programs which, if people act consistently and results are good, these start changing other internal programs.

♦ Effects of these changes will surely reproduce: By progressively going beyond the negotiation realm or differences at the workplace to encompass areas such as social, family, personal growth and quality of life.

CHAPTER 7

There's No Such Thing as a Free Lunch

7

Tell Me How Much You Are Willing to Risk and I'll Tell You How Much You Can Gain

For the purpose of examining human beings' usual behavior during negotiations, if we were able to classify individuals in a range going from "running the least possible risk" to "running the greatest risk", where do you think the majority would fall under? In which group would *you* be?

Your first answer would likely be "it depends" and it would be perfectly correct.

We could add that behavior is fluctuating and, according to the circumstances, the negotiation type as well, the moment in life and many other variables. This, too, is true.

However, the question points to a generalization, an intuitive answer, an opinion on how the majority of people behave in terms of taking risks at a given moment. Do the majority of people tend towards risk taking or, conversely, often act more conservatively?

What Moves People to Do Things?

There are only two motivational strategies.

Human beings are motivated to avoid pain, unpleasantness, discomfort, failure, stress, or any type of loss; or they are moved to achieve that which leads to pleasure, success, comfort, achievements, material goods, etc.

Both strategies are really useful and necessary since in every individual's life there are situations, people, places, actions and even ways of thinking that are best avoided, as well as places, people, situations, actions and thinking that are really worth having, being among or connecting to. We are all potentially endowed with both motivational means.

Considered as a whole, people are bound to be distributed along the continuum bearing different combinations of both strategies. However, considered individually, each person tends to use more of one of those methods mentioned earlier to manage his or her life.

Based on the type of family and community you grew up in, your education and cultural background there is a motivational approach that will influence your ability to take on more or less risk. Similarly, these thinking patterns or strategies appear in different contexts and influence your behavior with your couple, family and friends, at the workplace, and, of course, in negotiations.

I will rephrase the question: Which of the following motivations moves the majority of human beings?

♦ Avoid losing what you have and are fond of? or

♦ Achieve what you want and prefer?

How to Remove All Doubt

In order to answer this question less intuitively and more scientifically (though not accurately) when referring to negotiations, a study was conducted on the behavior of a group of people which enabled to express a statement with an acceptable degree of certainty.

Each introductory negotiation workshop run by CMI International Group opens with an exercise called "Pricing." This exercise is a sophisticated version of the classical "Prisoner's dilemma" created by Professor Roger Fisher and collaborators, at the *Harvard Negotiation Project*.

All participants play as members of the Board of Directors of two companies called Alba and Batia who sell oil to a country called Capita. These two companies have very poor relations and there is no communication between them.

This exercise enables Capita to sell oil at $10, $20 or $30 dollars per barrel. While both companies remain within that price range, neither will wipe out the other in the marketplace, neither will sell at a loss, and no competitor will be able to enter the market since transportation costs will render them less convenient. However, as shown in Table 7-1, each company's profit for every tax month depends on their pricing.

If both price equally, both will obtain equal profits; if they price differently, the one that sets the lowest price will obtain greater profits than the other team during that round. However, the explicit goal of the exercise is to obtain as much profit for your team regardless of the gain achieved by the other side.

Price fixed by **BATIA**

	$30	$20	$10
$30	$11 / $11	$2 / $18	$2 / $15
$20	$18 / $2	$8 / $8	$3 / $15
$10	$15 / $2	$15 / $3	$5 / $5

Price fixed by *Alba*

It is clear that the position where a team runs less risk of "earning more than the other company" is $10 and the riskier position is $30, though in no case are the organizations really unprofitable or have to put out money. According to the instructions, at the beginning of the previous tax month both companies priced each barrel at $20. Hence during the first round, each team has the chance to:

a. Continue pricing at $20.

b. Take on a conservative, competitive and short-term position by moving to $10.

c. Run the risk and obtain greater long term gains, playing at $30.

The Importance of Assumptions

Which is the logical choice in this first round? What does the choice depend on?

As expected, when this exercise is carried out with several universes (several pairs of negotiating teams), it is observable, though at different intervals, that some teams start off playing at $10, others $20 and yet others at $30.

When the exercise is reviewed among the participants, one of the questions posed to the group after observing the various ways of starting off is precisely the following: if some start at $10, others at $20 and yet others at $30, what would be the reasonable figure to start the first round with?

The type of move and therefore the rationale depends on the assumptions each group or Board of directors handles, especially those assumptions that prevail at the end.

If the group assumes that what is relevant is:

♦ Not to lose together with the other team; or win.

♦ To play short term.

♦ Not to run risks; protect yourselves.

♦ To think that the others are thinking as you are, and are not willing to run risks either, rather they prefer to go lower as soon as the chance arises.

Hence it is sensible to play at $10.

If the group assumes that what is relevant is:

♦ To make more money for their country, regardless of whether the other side also wins or gains more than they do.

♦ To play for the long term, even if it means losing in this round.

♦ To run the risk since uncertainty represents an opportunity to increase gains in the future.

♦ To think that the other side is thinking like them and want to run the risk considering the chance of greater gains.

Hence it is sensible to play at $30.

Generally $20 is the outcome of intermediate assumptions or the negotiated answer of a split group. So this exercise is an excellent opportunity to confirm or rule out the hypotheses regarding the behavior of the majority confronted with ambiguity.

The Majority Tends Towards... Statistics That Support Our Statements

This exercise has been practiced for years with hundreds of adults and young adults of both genders, from different social classes, varying degrees of education, profession or work, in different parts of the world, especially Europe, the US and Latin America.

Each exercise includes no less than three universes comprising two teams each which, in turn, include between three to five people, at the most.

Though the answer to the question on human behavior when faced with risk is founded on this long list, the study is based on analyzing the behavior of 263 groups and so comprises between 789 and 1,315 people.

In keeping with this analysis, 55.1% of the groups opted for the position of least risk during the first round ($10); 31.2% kept an intermediate response ($20) and only 13.7% chose a riskier position ($30), though all understood from the start that greater gains were obtained if both played at $30.

In answer to the ellipsis included in the subtitle of this chapter, according to statistical analysis of results and all experimental studies done in different parts of the world, the majority of people tend to move through risk avoidance as a basic motivational program; that is, they avoid unpleasantness, pain, discomfort, or losing what they have, and value anywhere from intangibles like acknowledgment to material goods such as money or belongings.

Coincidences?

Almost simultaneously to the writing of this chapter a report was published in the Uruguayan newspaper *El Pais* prepared by the consulting firm *CIFRA/ Gonzalez, Raga y Asociados* based on a representative sample of people from that country. The headlines read: "68% would choose to work in the public sector."

Those interviewed were asked the following question:

Suppose you are looking for work and you are offered two jobs. One is a public, not well paid position but with employment stability. The other is a better paying job in the private sector but with less employment security. Which would you choose?

Fifty nine percent (59%) of people in Montevideo and 80% of inland Uruguay population prefer a poorly paid public job to a private better paying job yet with less employment security. The same opinion is shared by 70% of those younger than 30. Only 9% of the overall interviewed think that liking what you do is the most important part of the job.

Incongruence as an Expression of Inner Conflict

An additional and interesting piece of data: when starting group work participants are instructed to decide in ten minutes' time, as a group, which will be their case goal, the strategy to achieve it, and, of course, the price for the first month.

When they begin to appraise the exercise, each group is asked to make public their goals and strategy.

All too often groups express incongruences such as "to achieve the greatest gains" as their goal and "running the least possible risk" as their strategy.

However, the incongruence articulated is not the most interesting point, rather that 88% of groups faced with this dilemma (a goal of improving profits and a strategy of running the least possible risk) decide for the least risky position, moving to $10 and showing through their actions how they ended up resolving the inconsistency.

Reaction as a Strategy

The other aspect that has been recorded as part of their strategy by groups pricing $10 is to "wait and see what the other side does." Almost 80% of groups that price $10 include to "wait and see what the other side does" as part of their strategy. As imagined, very often two teams pricing $10 confront each other waiting for several rounds just to "wait and see what the other side does" without realizing that:

- The other side of the other is us.

- The message they convey is almost never understood as a 'wait and see' behavior since they priced down from $20 to $10.

- They adopt a reactive behavior, waiting for the other side to act, hence placing responsibility and power on the others.

Alternatively, if the majority (63%) of those who decide to risk in the first round thus conveying a message of increasing the price to $30, get $10 from the other side they themselves become reactive and during the next round will go down to $10; or, the best case scenario to $20 hence forgetting or setting aside their initial goals of maximum joint gains.

Persevering on risk after the first initial setback seems to be less frequent, even less than taking it up from the start, in an uncertain situation. In this case, the factor that has a bearing on behavior is the second of the worst fears (and drives): fear (aversion) of a sure loss (or allegedly sure.) In summary, the risk-driven and perseverant people are a minority.

Everything Is Relative

The notion of risk and loss are relative since they depend on the point of reference taken. The latter could vary for different people in distinct situations or be manipulated according to circumstances.

What is considered gain or to gain is also relative to the point of reference taken, depending on the respective measure of success of the negotiations you are involved in.

If we take the "Pricing" exercise as an example, different groups may define success differently, resulting in distinct consequences to their strategies and actions. Success could mean:

♦ Win more than the other team.

♦ Not win less than the other team (not losing, the other side of the same coin.)

♦ To gain slightly more than the minimum allowable in the exercise.

♦ To gain more than was being gained till now (20/20.)

♦ To gain the maximum allowable in the exercise.

In fact, negotiators who begin the exercise at $10, as well as those who after pricing $30 in the first round and having received at $10 will lower their sale price on the following round, are surely thinking competitively. Generally, their point of reference is the money gained by the other team, though the exercise states that the other side's gains are really not important.

If you examine the profit table once again, you will notice that what the majority of the teams perceive as losing is really gaining less than the other side.

The truth is that they also make money since it is impossible to achieve a negative outcome in this exercise.

Conversely, if you do not compete with the other side you will appreciate that, for example, if you play $30 in the first round and receive $10, pricing at $30 in the second round and the other getting $10 leaves a $2 gain; lowering to $10 in the second round and receiving $10 from the other side results in a $5 gain.

It is clear there is no great difference in profits ($3) and no great risk is taken; except if the measure is the gain obtained by the other side.

It is also clear that no matter how small the difference in profits, you miss the chance of conveying the message of going 30/30 and gaining much more in the long term.

The feeling of loss by those who played $30 and got $10 can even be aggravated or increased if in addition to taking as a point of reference or thought framework the extra points earned by the other team, the supposed losers feel somewhat offended or that their good faith has been betrayed, deceived or surprised by the other party.

During negotiations, such emotions contribute to perceiving presumed losses, no matter how small, as insults hence justifying any kind of reaction.

Manipulating the Point of Reference

A few months ago I landed at the Miami International airport on my way back from Boston, on a flight arriving at 9:59 p.m. I was ready to take the 10:40 p.m. flight to Santiago de Chile arriving there at 6:30 a.m. because at 9:00 a.m. on the following morning I had to start a negotiation workshop with a prominent Chilean organization.

The arrival time gave me enough leeway to go to the hotel, shave, shower, change clothes and be ready to start the workshop on time.

Upon arrival at the airline counter, a kind employee announced over the loudspeaker that the flight to Santiago was delayed and that the departure time and reason for delay were unknown. A chaotic mental picture appeared in the minds of the majority of those sitting in the waiting room.

Almost immediately several people jumped out of their seats and crowded the airline counter. Amidst the uproar the employee announced that there was another flight departing at 12:30 a.m. and the airline would take care of rescheduling all passengers from the delayed flight, and try to move forward take off time, where possible.

Calmness ensued and everyone went back to their seats, many looking relieved, others satisfied and yet others recognizing their good fortune and commending airline management.

When observing what took place I asked myself what would have happened if the airline employee had said over the loudspeaker: "Attention passengers, I am sorry to announce the flight has been delayed for two hours."

In fact, that is exactly what happened to those of us who had a scheduled flight at 10:40 p.m.: a two-hour delay. However, everyone seemed calm instead of angry or bitter, even when not knowing whether it was just a company strategy to send off one full flight instead of two almost empty ones.

What happened? A change in the point of reference.

Compared to leaving and arriving on time —the airline's duty—, a two-hour delay would have been enough reason for protest; compared to the chances of not even arriving on the following day, a two-hour delay was praiseworthy.

For Those Who Did Not Participate in the "Pricing" Exercise, Here's a Quick Test

Suppose you travel to a country whose customs rules are somewhat strange. Like elsewhere in the world, when someone enters into a country after clearing immigration you are seen by a customs officer. What is a novelty in this case is the entrance system used by the officer.

He says: "To promote tourism, the government came up with this clever system I will now show you. See that big board right beside you with a red and a green light? Very well, those lights turn on when you press this button. At this time you can decide to go through customs without pressing the button, and in that case the government will give you $20 to spend freely, perhaps on the taxi to your hotel. If you decide to press the button, 25% of the times the green light turns on, and in this case the government will grant you $100; yet 75% of the times the red light turns on, and then you get nothing. In other words, you can have a sure win of $20 or bet on the lights. If you choose the latter, you'll have 25% chances of winning $100 and 75% chances of getting nothing. What do you choose?"

That is the question you must answer.

Now, after enjoying your stay in that country, when you are about to leave you find out that surprises are not over. After clearing immigration, you once again meet the customs officer and the light board awaiting tourists. When your turn comes around, the officer explains the clever new system again for leaving the country.

"You are already familiar with the light board, correct? Well then, now you may decide whether to go through without pressing the button, and in that case you will have to pay a departure tax of $20, or press the button. If you decide to press the button, 75% of the times the green light turns on and you will pass for free, and 25% of the times the red light turns on, then you will have to pay a $100 tax. What's your choice?"

Once again, that question goes for you.

According to experience and the great amount of research conducted, the majority of people vis-à-vis the first situation choose a safe gain of $20, motivated by the phenomenon of risk aversion, even when the expected value of the second option is $25, i.e. somewhat more than the $20 received for not participating.

The expression "expected value" is a concept related to probability calculation and decision tree tools.

If you decided to press the button, the expected value would be $25 since you have 25% chances of winning $100 and 75% chances of not getting anything, thus:

Expected value = (25%. $100) + (75%. $0) = $25

This value does not mean that during a specific turn you will receive $25. The latter value represents the amount of money you would receive on average in each opportunity if you pressed the button a considerable number of times (n.)

Hence, if you choose to ensure those $20, conservatively avoiding the chance of leaving without anything, you will be giving up the opportunity of gaining $100, less than the expected value. Yet if you are more inclined towards opportunities or if you wish to gain something, $100 would be very good but not $20, you would not give up your chance for the latter price.

The expected value obtained based on probabilities is then a point of reference for comparing the cost of acting to the benefit received under uncertain conditions, like in the exercise, in the absence of certainty.

Experience and research also show that the majority of people given the second situation (not press the button and pay $20 or press the button and have a one out of four chance of not paying) would choose to press the button and bet to avoid a safe loss, motivated by the so-called loss aversion phenomenon.

In summary, many more people are willing to bet (risk) in order to avoid losses than willing to bet (risk) to achieve gains (Khaneman and Tversky.)

Consequences of These Patterns

Any of these thinking and behavioral patterns make sense and have their meaning.

It is true that during an individual's lifetime there are positions, places, people, situations, actions and even thoughts that are dangerous, harmful and negative and are best avoided; as well as positions, places, people, situations and thoughts that are wonderful, positive and pleasant and best attained, pursued, contacted or actively attempted to take a hold of or experience.

It is also true that both mechanisms can lead to people's social success. Though a strategy based on achieving what you want (pleasure, prizes, goals) is clearly more appealing, there are well-known and frequent stories of individuals who have achieved fame and fortune motivated by avoiding in their adult life or avoiding for their children the pain they themselves suffered during their impoverished and unfortunate childhood.

Both mechanisms can be adequately combined for negotiating teams to achieve their goals more efficiently. When considering new and creative options to solve a complex problem it is best to ensure that these be explored by people who are geared towards achieving or searching (going towards...) It is critical to allow them to fully estimate achievable goals and limitations. When they have finished considering the odds, it is advisable to ask the avoiders to criticize ideas, state potential problems and what could hinder the achievement of suggested goals and objectives. This is the most productive way of using both strategies in **creative problem-solving; that is what negotiation is all about.**

Like in any other aspect concerning human beings, when considering large groups some individuals will place themselves at the end of a continuum; in this case, between maximum risk aversion and maximum willingness to take risks. Individuals located in or close to those ends will display behavior that is representative of their group, and almost always use the same motivational strategy to the utmost.

Taken to extremes, any of these thinking or behavioral patterns entails risks.

To risk it all without measuring consequences, naïvely trusting that all can be done and nothing may fail and that there is no need to appropriately prepare for a negotiation, may result in disastrous outcomes.

No other situation could be emotionally worse for corporate decision-making than euphoric mania, and **negotiations, too, deal with this issue: appropriate decision-making.**

However, negotiating when motivated by risk aversion and potential losses, the other extreme, may lead people to consider their measure of success as "not suffering any losses", or worse still "losing less than the other side."

Although it may sound contradictory, there are unperceived or uncalculated risks in the 'risk avoidance' or 'not losing' behavioral pattern.

Generally, negotiators become cautious when speaking of their interests and are reluctant to show creative problem-solving options for fear of being taken as commitments, and sometimes for fear of some other unimaginable problem arising ("I don't know what, but something bad may happen.")

Conversely, this thinking pattern prevents negotiators from making the slightest concessions since any of these could be considered a sure loss.

Exaggeration when measuring potential risk consequences may turn a negotiation into a "zero sum" game with poor outcomes ($10/$10) where it is impossible to expand possibilities and everyone involved fails to gain.

However, though all individuals have both motivational mechanisms available to them, combined in varying degrees, each person tends to resolve the majority of life situations using one of the two. As shown in the exercise statistics and in many pilot studies or research such as the consulting firm Cifra's work shows, the majority of people use the avoidance strategy. Some additional issues appear coupled to those earlier mentioned when using this strategy:

♦ Given that the motivational mechanism for acting is to avoid unpleasantness, their incentives for action are problems, negative situations and discomfort. When these conditions are perceived as being remote or not too threatening, motivation is lost until a problem becomes more compelling. Therefore, for those who use this strategy their motivation is typically cyclic.

♦ Since their motivational mechanism requires annoying situations, problems or discomfort, its users often suffer considerable amount of stress, anguish, angst and concern before acting; and sooner or later this may affect their physical and mental health. Knowing this may be the first step towards developing the appropriate sensitivity and learning how to respond to small stimuli without the trauma.

♦ Their attention is mainly focused on their dislikes, what they do not want and so for those using this motivational strategy it is not always clear what they really want and what their negotiation goal is.

Negotiating in these terms is like driving your car with the rearview mirror. By paying attention to pain, problem or discomfort avoidance you fail to pay attention to where you are going or your final destination.

Resuming Flexibility and Balance in Decision-Making

Almost all corporate futurologists predict, among other things, that forthcoming times will demand from negotiations and other fields two conditions that are scarce: risk taking capacity and being proactive.

Yet it seems that the majority of people who follow those basic programs display the opposite tendency.

Into the future, where uncertainty and change are likely to be the most certain and stable situation, success will be awarded to flexibility and mastery in balancing out natural trends.

Balance or stability does not mean being in the middle; it is not a question of taking risks in 50% of all negotiations you are involved in and acting conservatively in the remaining 50%. Balance means to be able to respond with flexibility, using different modes, according to circumstances, the context and the people with whom you are negotiating. It means to have once again the full range of possible combinations predicted for the 'avoidance' and 'achievement' mechanisms.

In doing so you need to review and question some typical behavior patterns. Silently and compellingly they reply to some old problems (from way back), greatly generalized and which often are not even created by our own criteria, and non-applicable to a current specific situation.

Family sayings and proverbs, among others, are typical of such subtly imbedded paradigms from childhood and that continue to rule our actions throughout adulthood.

A bird in the hand is worth two in the bush; better the devil you know than the devil you don't know; and, when in doubt, refrain, are some examples certainly ingrained in the thinking underpinnings of the majority of avoiders. Many of these restraining generalizations were included into each individual's biocomputer much before people were able to question their universal validity; thus their greatest power lies in being invisible to the conscious mind.

Therefore, to resume decision-making control in negotiations, it is important to first know yourself, know which is your conscious tendency, your metaprogram, as well as the metaprograms of the other side, to really tap into this knowledge.

- ◆ Is there a trend to have aversion to risk, the unknown, potential losses and problems? (Trend to avoid.)

- ◆ Is there a tendency towards risk taking, looking for opportunities, exposing yourself to possible consequences and problems resulting from that attitude? (Tendency to obtain.)

- ◆ Is there an inclination to wait and see what the other side does to later react? (Reactive.)

- ◆ Is there a tendency to act proactively taking on responsibilities for the proposed model's consequences? (Proactive.)

- ◆ How do people you generally negotiate with behave regarding these questions?

Most certainly and intuitively it is easy to define which of these patterns or tendencies you most frequently respond to as well as those with whom you relate to or negotiate with (spouse, children, bosses, friends, collaborators, clients, suppliers, neighbors, etc.), especially if they fall into one of the ends relative to risk.

If each knows his or her predisposition, he or she will be in a better condition to balance it out, sometimes internally and individually; at others building a negotiation team to even out that trend and tap into the strengths of both; or seeking help, counsel or professional advice.

Conversely, if you know the tendency of those you normally negotiate with you will at least know how best to submit information and suggestions during negotiations to motivate them or have more chances of persuasion.

So if you were negotiating an option with an avoider it would be advisable to first show all the problems that would be avoided if the option is accepted, and then go on to possible benefits. Adequately showing the negative consequences of not reaching an agreement may also be part of an initial strategy.

Alternatively, in the presence of someone who is inclined to achieving what he or she wants, more than avoiding problems it is best to try persuading him or her of future benefits of the proposed option rather than trying to show, at least initially, the difficulties entailed if the decision is not to negotiate and stick to their alternative.

As a point of reference for negotiation preparation, progress evaluation and outcome, it is suggested to use a measure of success that avoids always answering with a typical tendency, old styles or that is moved solely by emotions; a measure that replaces points of reference that may be manipulated, or that lead to unsatisfactory results.

A good outcome means that what was negotiated:

♦ Is better than the best alternative to a negotiated agreement (BATNA), that is, it is better than what you could have done alone or with a different person.

♦ Satisfies your own, the other side's and third party interests acceptably.

♦ Is based on a creative option with much added value and leaving no money on the table.

♦ Nobody felt cheated and legitimacy, objective criteria and standards other than parties' will have been used to persuade.

♦ Generated a commitment that was real, clear, functional and operational where all participants know what to do or not to do, when and how, and will be able to carry it through.

♦ Used efficient, two-way communication.

♦ Improved the relationship between the parties making it easy to negotiate again with the same person.

Equally, it is recommended to reasonably reduce uncertainty elements from complex negotiations or decision-making through appropriate tools and advice since it is not necessary to rush and make a decision where it is convenient and feasible to gather information to help reduce uncertainty. The speed of decision-making in current markets has accelerated forcing people not to miss opportunities and resolve difficult dilemmas lacking all the data negotiators would have wanted; yet, taking risks unnecessarily is not acceptable either.

> *"With the aid of tools derived partly from statistical analysis, the theory of games and other branches of quantitative analysis, situations may be studied with enough time to speculate adequately."*
>
> Danny Ertel

Data contributed by a probabilistic analysis (as the airport customs vignette shows) often helps to structure that which is known and decrease the area of uncertainty. Though nothing has been able to — and probably never will— replace experience, common sense, criteria and intuition in negotiations and decision-making, it is necessary to consider "the value in knowing a little more" in each case. For more information on this topic, the following reading is suggested, *The Art and Science of Negotiation* and *Smart Choices* by Professor Howard Raiffa.

In any event, given complex negotiations it is important to strike a balance between investing time and money to gather information and the contribution of such information to decision-making.

In some cases, investing time and money will clarify the situation and benefit less risky decision-making; in others, it will only increase risk or add new ones.

> *"Invincibility lies in the defense; the possibility of victory in the attack."*
>
> SunTzu

> *"I would not select the kind of man who flees, neither a man who is willing to wrestle with a tiger without worrying about saving his life. I would certainly pick a man who considers the obstacle with due prudence and who would rather win through strategy."*
>
> Confucius

CHAPTER 8

THE OBSCURE PRINCIPLE
OF RECIPROCITY ·

Negotiating With a Wolf in Sheep's Clothing

August 1992. My first cousin, his wife, my wife and I decided to take some short vacations in one of the most beautiful places on earth: Cancun, Mexico.

We arrived at dawn on a charter flight. A few minutes later, enough to leave our luggage at the hotel room and don our swim suits, we were all sitting comfortably on lounges waiting for the first sun rays to shine bright and encourage us to take our first dip in the Caribbean waters.

Right before doing so, one of the hotel waiters approached us offering some drinks and food to eat. After taking the order, he asked if we were interested in visiting the ruins of Tulum and Chichen Itza and tour Xcaret. We answered we would love to because we had heard those were fantastic places to visit.

The conversation became interesting because that fellow advised us on how to do the visits, what type of vehicle to rent, where to do so, etc.; advice we later realized proved useful.

At the same time, he gave us some coupons to get discounts at the tourist agency and also for the car rental. However, the important part of the story is coming up next.

After generating a pleasant connection, the waiter said that as a courtesy the hotel wished to invite us to breakfast or lunch (our choice) during our stay and visit the facilities so we could later recommend to others if they were to our liking.

This was one of our first human contacts in Cancun, our first encounter with a very aggressive time share sale system, one of the most unfortunate time wasting experiences of our lives, and, personally, one of the clearest examples of collective bribery I have ever seen; though I did not purchase anything I fell victim to that system.

After we finished our "courtesy" breakfast, my cousins, my wife and I— and I don't know how many other fools— got into a series of endless rollercoaster exhibits of different room types and services, going through a cascade of salespeople whose experience and skills remarkably went in crescendo. The offers went from individual presentations to collective shows, where hundreds of people applauded the victims who supposedly bought one of the last three or four "bargains" that remained available.

With all this ado, a couple of hours of our short vacation had disappeared into thin air, leaving behind a bitter taste and some interesting teachings for the rest of my life, a teaching I should have learned from my elders when they used to say: "If it seems too good to be true, it probably is."

The Secret Spring

I hadn't recalled this episode in years until once, when reading a book on the plane I understood the psychological principles (inner programs) this ploy appealed to.

The book was *Influence* by R. Cialdini and the principle I wish to refer to and mentioned in the book is 'reciprocity'. According to Cialdini, when given a gift human beings are generically hardwired to feel obliged to receiving it, and, in turn, to reciprocate. In fact, in Portuguese, the expression for thank you is *obrigado* (obliged.) This principle of reciprocity has a deeper meaning than it seems.

Many anthropologists and ethologists seem to agree that this mechanism is one of the pillars of living in a society. In order to live together in a society you must cooperate and share and nobody would want to do so if when giving someone something you weren't almost certain to receive something in return. Technically, that "something in return" means something similar in value, usefulness or characteristics. For example, if a person invites someone to dinner a few times, logic and experience indicate it is likely that, except for a very special reason, at some point such hospitality must be reciprocated. If not done or no explanation is given, chances are the other person will feel upset.

This may partly explain why many regular customers at bars and taverns end their nights terribly drunk. If someone from the group of friends invites the first round of drinks, each of the rest feels he must correspond similarly and order his round for all. The degree of ultimate drunkenness is generally directly proportional to the number of group members.

The Effect Is Not Proportional

The power of this principle is such that it can sometimes be used to achieve (or try to achieve like in the story) a return or response that is different from its content and/or disproportionate in quantity or volume just by the initial gesture of the other side.

Sometimes it suffices for a waiter to ask in a kind voice: "Is everything all right? Was your meal tasty?" so that out of reciprocity one may occasionally double the tip.

On a different note, all too often people who work in sales departments, service or department heads, judges, and so on, are not allowed to receive any type of present from a client or supplier, etc., no matter how small. Whoever enforced that rule knows that one of the problems of accepting small gifts is that the effect of the reciprocity principle often has no direct relation to the size or value of the initial gift, which may apparently be negligible. Whoever enforced that rule may logically assume that enabling the acceptance of small gifts may sometimes be too costly.

A variation of solving the issue thus (not allowing the acceptance of gifts) is used by other companies where gifts received by some members are raffled or distributed among all in an effort to avoid reciprocity to the donor by any one person.

The Same Holds True for Concessions

Many may have asked themselves how come someone they consider a friend dared give their name to a door-to-door salesperson selling English courses over the phone or books from door to door.

Most likely, after disturbing him or her for a while, the salesperson may "concede" not to further insist on a purchase if given a list of a dozen prospects. The salesman then goes on to a second alleged concession accepting three or four names rather than a dozen which number was the first true goal.

The origin of the "betrayal" is that same reciprocity principle; a concession is repaid with another one. The sociological base is the same.

In order for objectives to materialize for a political, social, corporate, sports or other group or system, its members must make some concessions regarding their interests or individual aspirations which they most likely would not be willing to make if the reciprocity sense were not present to ensure the exchange.

Generalization: Foundations of the Principle

One of the universal processes the human brain operates with is generalization, the mechanism through which, given one or several experiences, a general rule is drawn acting as a thinking simplifier, a shortcut for quick decision-making. When faced with an equal or similar situation, the brain no longer needs to go through the whole thinking process in order to act; it does so in an abbreviated way.

In and of itself it is a wonderful mechanism without which life would be very complicated.

> *"Pass behind the cannons, and in front of horses. Keep close to the kitchen and far away from your superiors. Salute anything that moves and what lies still paint in white."*
>
> Recruit survival tips

Without generalizations life would be impossible; yet when you generalize you also run some risks. The first risk is to draw the wrong conclusions when a single experience unrepresentative of the whole is made into a wrong general rule ("once bitten, twice shy" or "one example will suffice to prove it".)

Someone who when negotiating with Asians for the first time fared poorly concluded: "It's impossible to negotiate with Asians, they're all inscrutable"; surely he or she is experiencing one of the constraints of this universal thinking process.

In contrast to the previous example, the other risk is that though the general rule created may be right exceptions are treated equally or there is no capacity to perceive, given a new situation, that you are dealing with an exception.

The reciprocity principle, like all generalizations, may ultimately cause problems in negotiations; especially when replying automatically and when being victimized through distorted use to manipulatively reap an advantage (exception) and not fulfill its intended purpose.

The term 'manipulate' may be defined as using a basically dishonest behavior or conduct to achieve what is wanted. Manipulation can be accomplished by making others feel guilty for doing or not doing something, or fearful of doing or not doing something, or indebted for something said or done (bribery.)

Clearly, the manipulation mechanism involved in the earlier example is bribery: giving something or making a concession for the other party to feel indebted and expecting a disproportionately larger and/or different benefit in return.

Bribery Is But a Wolf in Sheep's Clothing

Though in a negotiation any of the three or a combination of such mechanisms may be involved, bribery is probably the most subtle.

It is much more likely for someone to defend him or herself with defiance against those trying to inflict fear via threats or those who play as victims attempting to inflict blame, than against those who have (supposedly) received something, whether time, recognition, affection, information, material goods or some type of service.

Conversely, bribery schemes combine the power of all mechanisms, as disguised behind false generosity they appeal to the guilt people feel if they fail to reciprocate favors, and sometimes fear of the unknown consequences of not doing so. Therein lies its power and force.

You Must Exercise Caution

Some of the most widely used negotiation systems (tactical combinations) are based on the following mechanisms:

1. Favors and counts

Probably the standard-bearer since its explicit motto is: "I'll do you a favor if you do me a favor in return."
The Godfather, Mario Puzzo's famous novel immortalized by Marlon Brando is the archetypal representation of this system. Someone does somebody a favor and records it in a ledger waiting for the timely moment to get paid back for it, generally in a different and disproportionate manner.

Different areas in life are prone to these types of dealings but it is most frequently found in politics, not just among politicians, political parties or fractions but also among politicians and their constituents on a two-way street.

Risks

Without considering ethical and moral aspects of some negotiations carried out under this system, favors and counts have a basic problem regarding the measure or value allocated to each. The relationship often ends up being damaged since no legitimacy or objective criteria are being used that are alien to the will or whim of the parties, or to subjective perceptions each participant may have, or to frequent attempts to obtain disproportionate results for concessions made.

2. Hard positions

The basic principle of the traditional haggling negotiation implies to start off by asking much or offering little, depending on what side you are on, to later make a concession expecting a return from the other side. The aim is that in exchange for a concession (each will appear to have made a very generous and final one before abandoning the negotiation) try to obtain an equal or greater concession from the other side.

Risks

Results from bargaining are arbitrary, lack legitimacy criteria and often prevent negotiators from focusing on mutual gains; parties' interests remain unexplored and no options are created to generate added value. Communication is very poor and full of tactics, deceit and trickery about interests, limitations and possibilities each negotiator has. The haggling becomes a duel or tug of wills that ends up damaging the relationship or ruining what could otherwise be a mutually convenient negotiation. If materialized, it is not uncommon for one or both negotiators to subsequently feel cheated.

3. Courtship and extortion

Under this system, relationship and substance get mixed up in negotiations. The goal is to establish a relationship that allows some part of the substance to be obtained from the other side. Just as the "amiable" advice of our friend at the beach, they look for reciprocity that is not only different but also disproportionate.

In the medical setting all too often pharmaceutical labs have identified those physicians who are opinion leaders and use this tactic with them. In its simpler version, when a new drug is being released into the market and needs to be included in institutions' formularies for product dissemination, one of the best ways is through these physicians; since their opinions are highly regarded by fellow colleagues, labs take them overseas for product presentations with all expenses paid. These meetings of course include some comradeship parties and tourist visits that create a warm atmosphere or at least good disposition. In addition, sometimes funding is provided to help research work and materials donation for such purpose which sure enough includes the product itself as well as resources for publication.

Regardless of the product being good or bad, convenient or inconvenient, these "Trojan horses" within organizations make it very hard for hospital managers when negotiating the introduction of a product to resist the reciprocity battering of those previously favored; a relationship resorted to by the lab when the going gets tough.

Risks

The risk is connected to the fact of confusing matters and thus feeling obliged to exchange elements of the substance for the relationship. Too often legitimacy criteria are lacking in these circumstances and you could even lose sight of your own, the other side's and third parties' true interests, like in the medication case.

4. Peacemaking

Some negotiators use the mechanism inversely and bribe with the substance, that is, they make concessions or give in on the substance with the intent to start or rebuild a damaged or threatened relationship.

Risks

The greatest problem is that this system tends to reward bad behavior. The other side quickly learns that by threatening to break off the relationship a concession is made hence generating an extortion game where, like in the previous case, relationship and substance are confused and parties lose sight of negotiating on the merits and legitimacy criteria.

First Step: Spotting the Ploy.

The first and perhaps most important step to defend yourself against any type of manipulation or ploy is to be able to spot it.

There are two complementary ways of doing so: one is to rationally know it exists; that is the goal of this chapter. However, it often does not suffice to rationally know about the existence of something to perceive it. The other way of spotting it is through emotions and feelings. Numerous authors are revaluing the importance of emotions and physical sensations as a kind of red flag that warns against and prevents potential problems.

Many times it is instinct that warns us we might be victims of a ploy and although our intuition may be mistaken, nothing guarantees that reason be unfailing.

What is important is to supplement diagnostic mechanisms and use the one with the earliest warning.

How to Defend Ourselves

If during a negotiation you recognize a ploy and still have time to do something about it, here are some general recommendations:

Occasionally it is convenient to use good communication skills and describe the game assertively to stop the player by revealing what is happening and seek agreement on a different negotiation process.

In this case you should speak on your own behalf and not on behalf of others. Say what you think and feel is happening, using a hesitant tone without attribution of intent to the other side; not forgetting that:

1. Courtesy costs nothing but gains everything.

2. Though using a gentle inquisitive tone or even denial, the idea you want to convey will come out.

3. The reciprocity rule is the true enemy in this game and not the person who makes use of it.

For example, I could have said something like: "I'm sure that by serving us so kindly you don't intend to make me feel obliged to tour the hotel facilities, right? (Because if that is the case, I won't accept it.)" The other party will understand though with various reactions going from acceptance, to confusion and even anger (true or false.)

Conversely, you can prevent the mechanism from going off altogether and, just like in many organizations' sales departments, make the decision not to accept any gift whatsoever from those with whom you negotiate. In this case what you most likely must negotiate is to apply this rule. The problem with such decision is that you might fail to distinguish honest from dishonest services and a legitimate concession from a ploy.

Another possibility is to search for and use legitimacy criteria as a reciprocity shield and measure, where applicable. Treat gifts received for what they truly are and not for what they represent. The reciprocity principle says that a gift or favor must be returned with another gift or favor; yet manipulation should not be returned with a favor. (Next time I would accept the breakfast offered and would add that if he visits my city one day, I would gladly invite him to a similar breakfast.)

When recapping on the true interests of the situation you will discover that oftentimes they do not match the gifts you are receiving.

Exploring alternatives to achieve those interests will sometimes help not to fall into the game. Always separate the issues from the substance (money, material goods, dates, conditions, concessions, etc.) and those related to the relationship (emotions, reason, understanding, trust, acceptance, respect, etc.); it is an invaluable guide in these situations.

Lastly, one of the most important recommendations is to learn from each experience by asking yourself: Knowing what I now know, would I do it again?

If the answer is no, then ask: What would I do differently?

CHAPTER 9

Negotiation: Ritual, Activity or Psychological Game?

9

How Do You Manage Your Negotiation Time?

Time Structuring: One of Our "Primal Needs"

One of human beings' basic needs is time structuring.

The way in which each one structures time daily and throughout life is a variable combination of six possibilities.

♦ Withdrawal

♦ Rituals

♦ Activities

♦ Pastimes

♦ Psychological Games

♦ Intimacy.

During a negotiation, including preparation time, participants may go through any and sometimes all of these time management modes.

What is certain is that results of such negotiations will be better or worse, according to how they are used or avoided, the time devoted to each, the sequence in which they are used and how they adapt to the situation.

Although the terms "structure" or "manage" sound like a rational distribution of hours available each day, in this case they refer to the way in which we fill our available time to provide us with enough "vital stimuli."

Vital stimuli can be understood as the charge of our biological battery, without which we would not have the energy to function.

At each moment of the day we find ourselves in any one of the six time distribution modes. Each is distinct from the other in terms of emotional commitment, among other things; thus, the quality and quantity of stimuli received or exchanged also differ.

Following an arrangement of increasing emotional commitment, here is a simple description of each of these time structuring modes.

♦ Withdrawal

Often, when alone, we are self-absorbed in our thinking and inner dialogues. Studying, planning, reading a novel and listening to music are frequent situations of withdrawal and yet not necessarily. Other times, though surrounded by people, we are physically present but mentally absent; our mind is elsewhere or we are daydreaming. In both cases we withdraw.

♦ Rituals

Rituals are one of the common characteristics of all human beings, and some are transmitted generation after generation. From the simplest everyday greetings to the most complicated and infrequent ones such as the crowning of a king ceremony; they all follow a set of repetitive and predictable norms. Once a ritual is triggered, each upcoming step is known as well as the ending. Perhaps because of this nature, its value in terms of social stimuli is poor, though greater than the withdrawal mode value. However, on account of their frequency rituals enable a great number of exchanges.

♦ Activities

Whenever we are involved in the process of achieving a goal or attaining something, we are dealing with an activity. Even if it means brushing our teeth, playing chess or a soccer match, whether carrying out the hardest negotiation or the riskiest working plan of our career; if the goal is to do or achieve something, we are in the activity mode. Stimuli (recognition) resulting from activities are generally more powerful than those of rituals and are basically related to results obtained. Although a job may be the stage for any of these modes of time structuring, generically speaking activities should be the salient mode in this context.

♦ Pastimes

Often two or more people pass their time talking about something without any intention to resolve a problem. Though sometimes they seem to be fixing the world, pastime conversations are superficial and revolve around a more or less entertaining common theme.

Social meetings and endless bar talks are especially fit for time structuring in this mode, yet sometimes a supposedly work meeting (activity) may become a pastime. It is important to underscore that though we often use this term for sports, board games or computer games —the goal in each being to achieve (do) something— they are included in the activities category. Perhaps what is most important about pastimes is that they enable participants to determine with whom they can engage in psychological games.

♦ Psychological games

So called because they are similar to mathematical games or games of chance. All psychological games have a set of rules, a starting time, a development stage (where each player must alternately play for the game to move ahead) and a scheduled ending where the "settling of scores" occurs. What is especially typical of these games are players' hidden though unconscious motives. They entail a set of transactions (social exchanges) apparently acceptable at rational and social levels, but comprising double messages; that is, a series of underlying hidden messages at a psychological level. These are critical elements in determining the final predictable outcome or "benefit," its ultimate purpose.

Behind a socially acceptable facade, all psychological games include a concealed trap whose purpose —dishonestly yet unconsciously— is to take advantage of the other side's weakness. Though the term may indicate fun, outcomes are never fun; they range from a simple bitter aftertaste to jail or the morgue.

♦ Intimacy

Those who structure their time in this way share feelings, emotions and perceptions and do so openly, trustingly, and taking risks at the same time. There are no hidden agendas; nobody is willing to take advantage of the other side or their weaknesses.

Relations are straightforward, lacking hypocrisy or falsehood and, though not always nice to feel (for example, being close to someone who lost a loved one), it brings out the best in us and also the best in others. The heartfelt embrace of two friends' reunion, a mother comforting her hurting child, a successful working team operating through that feeling of perfect complementarity; all of these are examples of such relationship. A distinction and clarification should be made between sex and intimacy. Sex is a physiological activity, it could take place under the withdrawal, ritual or activity mode, it could also be a pastime, be part of a psychological game or happen within intimacy boundaries. Just as sex can take place without intimacy, intimacy can occur without sex.

Structuring Time in Our Negotiations

A negotiation, as so many other frequent and complex situations in life, is a good venue for various combinations of time structuring modes to appear.

Different combinations will depend much on the context and type of negotiation at a given time, but will also be dependent on the personality of each party involved; personality meaning the way in which people generally think, feel and behave to satisfy their needs.

In almost all negotiations there are moments of *withdrawal.*

During preparation, even if done in groups, we often need —and it is advisable— to take some time out for personal reflection and insight. Listening to our inner dialogues, sometimes resulting from harsh internal negotiations is often very beneficial.

Other times, being able to explore our real interests requires some time to ourselves.

During negotiations per se, we might also need some time for withdrawal, especially if we perceive we are getting involved with emotions that are not convenient for our own purposes, or our gut feeling is sending us a message we still cannot make out.

Lastly, a good results evaluation will benefit from some time set aside for personal thought when we can rationally and methodically do a checklist of our actions as well as an internal evaluation of our emotions and feelings as to the process used and results obtained.

Some negotiations are all about boring *rituals.*

Though almost all negotiations include some sort of ritual — at least greeting rituals— others are solely rituals.

A typical haggling negotiation applies fully to the definition of this mode of structuring time. It has a series of guidelines and pre-established rules, once it starts it unfolds, follows known steps and the end is predictable.

The buyer or seller starts out with an "offer" which, if accepted, becomes a commitment and, overtly or in disguise, threatens with the alternative: not to buy or not to sell. The other side acts similarly. After the first offer, and unless it was outrageous or offensive to the other negotiator, there follows a second higher or lower offer, depending on whether it originates from the buyer or seller, disclosed by each as the "final offer." The other side acts similarly.

Hence a series of moves will ensue where ritual participants will get closer to a possible agreement on price through successive "final offers," "final-final offers" and "*the* final offers," including in each the threat to leave and buy elsewhere or sell to another potential buyer; both often non-existent.

Exciting to some, boring to others, this ritual is the most frequently seen in short-term negotiations and, perhaps, the only possible way of negotiating if we want to purchase handcrafted articles during our vacations or bargains in a flea market; yet it is absolutely inconvenient for complex negotiations, i.e. negotiations that replicate over time including multiple parties and issues.

Many negotiations open spaces for *pastimes*, those moments for participants to talk about trivial matters. Often, in lengthy negotiation preparations, when negotiators are trying to create a relationship and especially if they have no well-thought out plan on how to build it, they may possibly spend time on pastimes.

In these cases, talking about trivial matters eases the tension and helps to get to know each other.

Other times, a group meets to prepare for a negotiation and because they lack organization skills, or a method, or just because they become tired, they engage in pastimes.

Lastly, past negotiations are often the subject matter of conversations between fellow colleagues, friends or relatives. Although there is nothing inherently wrong with them, unfortunately these pastimes are a poor substitute for a real evaluation. The intent in these cases is not to learn from successes and failures, rather just to comment on, comfort yourself or brag about what happened.

Occasionally, during negotiations one or more *psychological games* take place or the negotiation can be just a move, part of a greater psychological game.

All psychological games need at least two players, though they may be played by many, who, from their different roles, develop distinct stages that are included in those games. The game is sequential and progresses if one of the player's move (invitation) is answered by the other. Conversely, the game stops if there is no answer.

As in fishing, psychological games generally consist of the following:

a) A *bait*: a worm on the hook is the hidden and ulterior part of the stimulus aimed at "hooking on" to the other side's vulnerable or weak spot.

a) A *weak point* and *discredit*: the fish "thinks" it will be easy to eat the prey by denying (discrediting) aspects of reality like the hook and line.

b) A *response*: the fish responds to the invitation of the bait hooked through its weakness and gets drawn into the game by biting the hook.

c) A *change*: when the fisherman sees the buoy sinking, he shifts attitude and pulls the rod upwards, thus the apparently weak worm reveals the sharp hook and the fish becomes the victim rather than the victimizer in the story.

d) A *pseudo-benefit* or settlement of scores: for the fish it is death; for the fisherman, the joy of having caught the fish, except if when eating it he swallows a fish bone and becomes the victim instead of the victimizer.

For psychological games to be considered as such they must have:

♦ A series of acceptable transactions at a social or conscious level.

♦ A set of more powerful and important hidden and ulterior messages at a psychological or unconscious level.

♦ A predictable ending which is the ultimate aim.

♦ Basically, a psychological game is dishonest, though unconsciously, since it aims at achieving its goal through manipulation, not overtly; it is repetitive, it does not generate a real solution or satisfy the needs or interests of the players, and it is dramatic on account of the strong degree of emotions and role changes that occur.

Some of them, first-degree games, remain "in-house" and are socially accepted.

Second-degree games transcend close ties or the family setting and bring about damage at a social or commercial level; whereas third-degree games are really serious with high intensity and end results lead to court, jail, the hospital or even the morgue.

Participants assume any of the following three roles: Persecutor, victim or rescuer.

These three roles described by E. Berne where represented by Karpman in the shape of a triangle, known as the **Drama Triangle**.

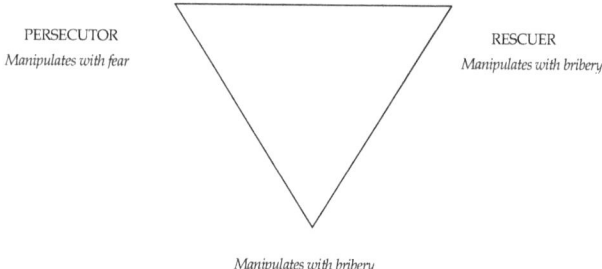

PERSECUTOR

Manipulates with fear

RESCUER

Manipulates with bribery

Manipulates with bribery

Each player representing one of the three roles in this game seeks to achieve something by manipulating others using fear, guilt or bribery.

Persecutors manipulate using fear since they need to be feared.

Victims manipulate using guilt because they need to be persecuted or rescued.

Rescuers manipulate using bribes since they need to be needed.

However, each player starts the game in a specific role. Psychological games require role switching in successive moves. Hence, someone who started off as persecutor or rescuer will shift to victim or from victim to persecutor, and so on.

By way of example I will present two psychological games. The first is a very common day-to-day game taken from Doctor R. Kertesz and originally described by Berne, the so-called "Yes, but" game, and the second is an example of a real negotiation case.

Psychological games can last a few minutes, years, a life span or even be passed down to the next generation.

Example 1

In a group, Mrs. X says: "I can't stand my husband any longer, I don't know what to do with him." (This seems to be an adult and rational stimulus at a social level yet at an ulterior, hidden level the message conveyed is of hopelessness and a concealed request for help, putting down her own ability to find a solution, thus assuming a victim role. Hopelessness is the bait to "hook" the rescuer from within the group members.)

Mr. Y responds, since his weakness is helping others and giving advice to people to "rescue" them: "Why don't you get a divorce?" (Though at a social level it seems to be a question or suggestion, at a concealed level it puts down Mrs. X's capacity to solve the problem; in addition, it encloses some piece of advice that was not expressly asked for. This is the response phase.)

Mrs. X answers in an apparently rational way providing data not evident at first: "*Yes, but* my children are too small and I don't have a job." There is a clear concealed rejection of advice given and the change begins to take place.

Other parties to the meeting or even Mr. Y continue providing new ideas or suggestions which will be systematically rejected using the formula: "*Yes, but...*"

Mrs. X has switched from victim to persecutor and the rescuers have started to feel they are the victims of the game.

After a more or less lengthy series of transactions, Mrs. X might defiantly close by saying: "You see, nobody can help me."

As a final result, Mrs. X will have this feeling of triumphalism (or false triumph) thinking deep inside that nobody is going to tell *her* what to do; and the confused or enraged advisers perhaps think it is useless trying to help someone.

Example 2

Sean Brown and Frank Morton first met at a project the former had developed for International Shoes Inc., through ICC Consultants.

Brown was a well-known and prestigious technician and a faculty member who had served as director in IT centers for several large organizations.

Morton had earned a degree in management, was very smart and had an amazing work capacity, but felt somewhat frustrated because he was unable to finish his engineering studies. He used to work for an important international consultancy firm which he left to join ICC.

The work performed on the project was very successful.

Once the initial project was completed, Brown went on to other projects serving as independent consultant, simultaneously developing a new computer program called Praxis which was created as a powerful mathematical calculus simplification tool, applicable to almost any engineering or construction work.

Meanwhile, Morton continued working for ICC Consultants growing in prestige and power until he was fired due to differences with the company Chairman.

He then created his own consultancy firm and started working for a prominent bank. Shortly after he became director of the IT department and after two-years' time he became Vice President.

A year later Morton resigned from his position claiming that banking business was immoral.

Once again out of work he created a new consultancy firm, Practical Marketing (PM) and he went back to working with another significant bank from which he was fired, once more due to differences with the organization's Chairman.

Meanwhile, Brown had completed the development of Praxis, a program in which Morton originally did not believe.

During that time, Brown and Morton had had a few professional contacts and a not too close personal relationship since their lifestyles were quite different. Morton was arrogant, self-centered, spent large sums to decorate his offices, on cars, cell phones, etc., as well as on vacations and entertainment while Brown was rather conservative and thrifty.

When visiting Brown's offices, a few months prior to this last incident, Morton had devoted some hours to learning about Praxis. Given his current situation, he asked Brown to help him out by granting him the distribution of Praxis.

In its infancy, Praxis was being distributed by a small company but only in the microprocessing field. At that time the AS400 was to be released, so Brown decided to grant Morton the chance of product distribution.

No agreement or contract was signed as they both knew each other.

Sales were very good during the first year, and even better on year two, hence Morton became responsible for almost the entire Praxis market.

Overall, adding programs and maintenance services Morton sold over 15 million dollars in the third year generating very good dividends for Brown.

Simultaneously, one of Brown's partners was trying, unsuccessfully, to develop the European market. Since they were very keen on introducing Praxis and its services they accepted Morton's proposal to work that market too.

In this occasion, Morton requested an exclusive sales representative agreement for that country stating that it was required for securing potential local partners; thus he created Praxis Inc., based in London.

In line with his style, all Morton's companies displayed exponential growth in number of people, size of facilities, luxurious furniture, cars, etc., all of which Brown was not fond of.

Moreover, Brown had started to notice some changes in Morton.

Morton was not getting along well with his wife and everybody knew about his crazy love affair with one of his young assistants.

Morton's relationship with Brown was also changing and, contrary to certain initial admiration and recognition of his intellectual capacity, some tense moments were now becoming more frequent, like the one that took place during the company's yearly meeting with clients where Morton got up from the table annoyed and left without any explanation.

However, as business was doing well, when Morton suggested signing a national distribution agreement for unlimited time and with exclusive representation for his own country, Brown agreed almost blindly, even when no sales goals were established in the contract.

Things changed from that moment on.

The organization created in Europe was not operating well and payments Practical Marketing used to make regularly and timely were delayed and even discontinued for months amounting to a debt of over $400,000 dollars.

When Brown demanded payment, Morton claimed he was straightening out some matters both from a fiscal and legal standpoint and that Brown need not be concerned because the money was put away safely.

During one of Brown's trips to London, Morton caused an annoying and violent incident in a restaurant regarding the designation of the CEO of Praxis Inc.; a second episode took place at the international airport with an airline officer on account of flight cancellations due to bad weather conditions.

Yet another more violent situation occurred during the international software fair held in Amsterdam; Brown expressed his disagreement on a very expensive stand Morton had set up at the fair. Morton not only became enraged throwing objects against the wall, but also threatened to destroy the stand when fully operational during the fair.

As matters worsened and Brown was especially interested in doing good business deals and doing the right thing in the European market, he decided to ask Morton to purchase Praxis Inc.; and Morton accepted.

The sale contract was signed for 10% of the first three year sales plus the $100,000 dollar promissory note settlement with one year maturity which Morton had requested at a bank. Thus Brown would take immediate administrative and commercial control of the London-based company.

Several months later, as debts generated by Practical Marketing were not being settled and hoping to finish with the relationship, Brown decided to demand payment under penalty of voiding the contract as provided in the terms.

Morton then decided to repay part of the debt but months later Brown was forced to demand payment again and received, in turn, a profit and loss account from Morton where, according to his estimates, Brown owed him $75,000. When the 60-day deadline for contract voidance was due, Brown decided to open up a new local distribution company, and though over a year had gone by from contract signature for Praxis Inc. he also decided not to pay what he owed Morton for the purchase as he believed Morton's debt with Brown was higher.

In addition, once the $100,000 loan settlement deadline was due, the lending Bank claimed the sum of $50,000 as collateral deposited by Morton.

Morton then filed two legal claims against Brown.

He decided to file a suit against Brown in the country of origin for breach of the Praxis Program exclusive and unlimited distribution contract through Practical Marketing. Moreover, Brown received a written demand from Gordon & Gordon Law Firm in London, for breach of Praxis Inc. sale contract, under penalty of a legal suit in that country, which would seriously go against Brown's long-term interests in the European Economic Community.

To add insult to injury, Brown finds out that all Praxis clients in its country of origin have just received an offer by e-mail from an unknown address in Europe requesting the delivery of the original version of Praxis in order to remove the protection that prevents program duplication in exchange for a very convenient sum.

Case Analysis

If we analyze what happened from a psychological game perspective, we may notice that the narrative, with slightly changed data from the real case, has all the elements of a game.

It has a *bait*: Morton, a seeming victim in disgrace (fired and without a job) asking for help.

There is a *weak point*: the request "hooks" with Brown's rescuer side of wanting to help, but also with his persecutor side: without much ado and no investment he could get someone who is in need, smart and a good worker to start developing a market for a still not well-known product without having to sign a contract and generating no commitments.

It has a *disqualifying* element: Brown ignored reality and much data that clearly spoke to the type of person Morton was. Dismissals for issues with organizations' authorities, his resignation for no compelling reason, his habits and their very distinct work styles were not considered when the relationship started.

It contains a *response*: Brown bites the hook by signing an almost blind contract for an indefinite period granting Morton exclusive representation over Praxis without even setting any commercial goals whatsoever *(see Figure I.)*

There are several *changes*: Once the contract is signed things change and regular payments as well as profits disappear giving rise to employment and personal problems which changes Brown from a rescuer (or persecutor) into a victim and Morton shifts from apparent victim to persecutor *(see Figure II.)* Later on, Brown takes the distribution away from Morton and fails to pay the sale contract for Praxis Inc., thus shifting from victim to persecutor, and Morton from persecutor to victim *(see Figure III.)* Lastly, Morton files a suit against Brown in both countries and it is unknown whether he is responsible or not for those e-mails, so once again he shifts from victim to persecutor and Brown from persecutor to victim *(see Figure IV.)*

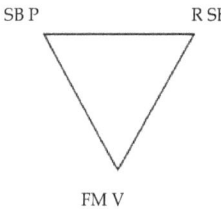
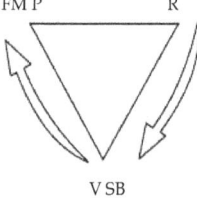

No. I - Initial situation

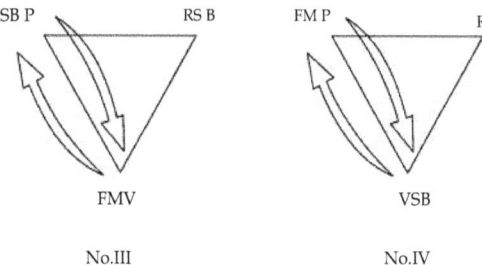

No.III   No.IV

Both are now involved in lawsuits and disputes using up huge amounts of energy and vital time (work, social, family, etc.), absorbed in intense emotions which could be considered part of the *pseudo-benefits* of the game (lose-lose.)

However, unless an adult ego state decision of any of the participants arbitrates, this game is not over and the *final settlement of scores* lies ahead.

This is clearly a second-degree game, greatly transcending the social and commercial levels and, unfortunately, if participants are not able to unhook themselves, it may end up as a third-degree game.

Finally, in very few occasions are negotiations the stage for *intimacy* transactions.

This is not a typical negotiation trait but rather a general life trait since intimacy is perhaps one of the most desired yet mostly feared situations by humans for the emotional commitment it entails.

In addition, in negotiation the concept is easier to intuitively grasp and to explain. I believe the best way to convey it is through an example.

Some months ago I participated in a long and difficult negotiation with two groups who were looking to merge to carry out consulting work.

One of the parties to the negotiation had created and successfully led our group for about three years and was now being invited to participate in the creation of a new group together with other four consultants under very convenient terms for his interests, skills and capabilities.

One of his goals, and ours too, was to try and merge both groups which was theoretically viable and attainable in practice.

After long hours of amiable yet arduous negotiations, incompatible differences in issues regarding ownership and especially what that meant in terms of personal and professional recognition of each group's members, we concluded there would be no agreement.

Articulating this into a sentence was the trigger for one of the moments of greatest intimacy I have ever had a chance to participate in during negotiations. During the short silence that ensued the conclusion we heard sobs from one of our former companions who was beginning to grasp the reality of the loss.

Regardless of all the good that awaited him in the new group there was the pain of parting with something he himself had created, leaving behind old friends and fellow workers he himself had chosen, as well as shared efforts and dreams.

A few seconds later, one of the members of our group burst into tears too, and those of us who did not cry, tears filled our eyes. Silence befell on the meeting like a heavy mantle that pushed us against our seats and we remained motionless. After a few minutes which felt like ages came a heartfelt embrace with our friend, and without further ado the gesture sealed the meeting.

A Recommended Distribution

There is no such thing as an exact recipe on how time should be distributed whether in negotiation or other things in life. However, we are able to make some general useful recommendations.

◆ Firstly, life, and not only negotiations, must be free from psychological games. Though it is feasible in other time management modes to distinguish between positive and negative usage, this is not so with psychological games. For example, we can say there are good and bad rituals. A good ritual may be a polite greeting in the morning or waltzing at a wedding. A negative ritual can be when a sect ends up with the death of one or several of its members, as took place several times in the past. Conversely, psychological games by definition and by results obtained are negative for all participants, no matter the degree and duration.

◆ Every negotiation requires some time for withdrawal during any of its stages (preparation, negotiation, and results and process evaluation.) If overused it can deprive us of the invaluable contribution of teamwork.

♦ Time devoted to social rituals are necessary for good relationships and communication, thus it is indispensible to consider this aspect when negotiating with people from cultures that are very distinct from ours, for example negotiations between Westerners and Asians. However, we consider it is not convenient to participate in bargaining type of rituals when dealing with a complex negotiation, not only because results are poor compared to those of interest-based and principled negotiations, but also as it is a ritual once started it is very difficult to leave or "unhook" from and restart via a different avenue.

♦ An apparently trivial conversation, when timely and relevant in terms of the subject, helps to relax, relieve tensions or generate a good relationship between negotiation participants. In this case, we recommend planning pastime dialogues ahead, where possible. Often, it is in the opening conversation, during those few initial seconds or minutes, where the fate of our communication and our relationship is at stake; at times even the entire negotiation is. Pastimes are inadequate when used ill-prepared, when not knowing what to say, or when they replace a good negotiation process. Nothing is truer in negotiations than the saying "a closed mouth catches no flies." We have all seen negotiations come to a standstill and occasionally spoil definitively as a result of an untimely conversation on a subject not relevant to the negotiation.

♦ Beyond what was said about intimacy, the recommendation is do not be too careful; it does not happen that often and when it does, it will do you a lot of good. Whether pleasant or unpleasant to experience, it will make you feel human.

♦ It is highly recommended to spend most of negotiations on activities. Results are statistically better when negotiators spend the majority of their time on preparation, negotiation and evaluation guided by clear objectives and following a strategy and methodology to attain them. In addition, using a method (our Harvard model or other) will help you not to get involved in psychological games or any inappropriate time distribution mode.

♦ Lastly, principled negotiation is, once again, our strongest general recommendation.

If in Spite of That…

No one is more at risk of falling into the trap of a psychological game than the person who is ill-prepared for a negotiation, without clear goals and lacking a strategy to attain them; and in spite of attempting a principled negotiation, nobody is exempt from discovering at a given time that he or she is faced with or involved in a psychological game.

The question then is: How do you get away from that situation?

This reminds me of a patient at a psychiatric institute who asked Doctor E. Berne: "How do I get out of this place?" "And how did you manage to get in?", replied the doctor.

Our best recommendation, as in the previous case, is: avoid getting in.

♦ Firstly, use the tool, think in terms of games, ask yourself if the funny feeling in your stomach is just tension because you are facing a complicated case, or is it your gut feeling warning you of a trap.

♦ Acknowledge your weaknesses. You know yourself enough to tell what role you typically use to get involved in the drama triangle, whether in negotiations or day-to-day life, and what bait you generally bite into. Discovering it now will help you to timely predict or recognize it, and enable you to use other more creative and efficient options to obtain what you want.

♦ If you recognize when someone is "inviting" you to play a game or that he or she is already in one of their moves, you may:

a) Expose or reveal the game. Assertively put on the table what we observe, share information and, perhaps with the triangle diagram, explain what is happening, addressing others in first person and without attributing intention to the other side. It is possible to let others know how we feel and even suggest to follow a different option.

b) When we cannot confront the situation because it is not convenient due to power imbalance or because doing so would be shameful to the other side, or because we have tried it before and did not work, an option is to continue with the game. Once you have discovered the game or invitation, without hooking onto your weakness, pretend acceptance and as soon as you can, evade the game.

c) Evading the game is another possibility. We can leave if necessary, ignore the invitation and change subject or shift to another element. For example, if somebody is manipulating the relationship from a victim role, you may separate the substance from the relationship and shift to exploring or talking about interests and legitimacy criteria.

An example dialogue:

The owner of the company when an employee asks for a raise:

"Why are you doing this to me? I was the one who got you this job when you were a kid and taught you everything you know. I feel badly, I thought I was like an uncle or father to you. I see I was wrong, you haven't the slightest consideration for me." (Clearly manipulative from the victim role, inviting the rescuer in the other side.)

Employee:

"If at some point I led you to believe that I don't care about our relationship or that I'm not thankful to you for all the knowledge you shared and everything you've done for me, I'm sorry, I do care and I will always be thankful to you. However, I believe we must separate our relationship from my asking for a raise. The raise I am asking has to do with my performance at work and, in asking for it, I am considering what others in the same position are earning, and who have joined the company after I did. I only want to be treated at the workplace just like others are being treated." (Assertively evades, separating relationship issues from substance and shifting from the relationship element to his interest in the raise and the criteria he is considering for such a request.)

Our Final Recommendation: Be Unreservedly Constructive

Even when the other side acts emotionally, balance out emotions with reason.

In doing so, rely on good preparation work, use principled negotiation and a methodology to support it.

Even if they do not listen, listen to them and ask them questions. The information obtained, both content and shape, will be critical to your persuasion strategy.

Even when you are misinterpreted, try to understand them. Remember that the only way of persuading others is by understanding how they perceive things and process data so you can later change it.

Even when they reject your point of view without considering it, respect their right to differing opinions. Accept them as worthy of your consideration.

Even when they try to deceive you, be worthy of trust. We do not recommend trusting naïvely; we recommend being reliable. Experience shows that the latter condition is very valuable at the time of negotiating.

Even if they try to manipulate you, be open to persuasion. Refuse invitations to participate in psychological games. Seek to persuade using objective criteria, alien to parties' will, and remember that there are few things that are more persuasive than being open to legitimate persuasion.

You are now probably thinking about me: "These suggestions will get him into heaven."

If you believe in heaven, it might be an added value for following these suggestions; but I share my suggestions because they are suitable and convenient.

In our opinion, *the true power in negotiations* lies in knowing how to:

♦ Look for and develop a good *alternative*, that is, know what to do to satisfy your interests if there is no agreement; and having thought about how to persuade the other side.

♦ Discover *interests* (what people really need) underlying positions (what people say they want); both yours, and the others' and third parties' in order to satisfy them.

♦ Separate the process of deciding from the process of inventing. Allow yourself and allow others to be creative when inventing *options* for possible agreements that "expand the pie."

♦ Use sound *legitimacy criteria* to persuade and defend yourself from dirty manipulations and tactics used by others.

♦ Engage in intelligent, clear, functional and operational *commitments* as late as possible in the negotiation process, only after having thoroughly explored interests, options and objective criteria.

♦ Generate two-way *communications* where everybody is heard and understood.

♦ Create a good *working relationship*, that is, know how to resolve differences politely and assertively.

CHAPTER 9

And What Does That Mean?
It Depends

Reframing: The Art of Living

An old Chinese Taoist story tells about a farmer who lived in a poor village. He was considered very fortunate because he had a horse to plow the land and also a means of transportation. One day the horse ran away.

The neighbors came to his farm to pay their respects for the terrible loss, but after listening for a while the farmer only said, "It depends."

A few days later the horse returned home with two wild horses.

The neighbors became excited at the farmer's good fortune but the farmer only said, "It depends."

On the following day, the farmer's son went to ride one of the wild horses; he was thrown from the horse and broke a leg. All the neighbors felt distressed for the farmer's ill fortune yet the farmer once again only responded, "It depends."

On the following week, a troop of soldiers came to the village to recruit young men for the army. The farmer's son was not drafted because of his broken leg. When the neighbors congratulated the farmer on his good luck, the farmer answered, "It depends."

Facts and Meanings

Nothing has an implicit meaning in the world. The meaning of any fact depends on who perceives it, from what angle it is perceived, through the sieve of what beliefs and paradigms as well as how it is processed internally.

What does it mean when you are walking down the street and bird droppings land on your shoulder? For some it is misfortune, and chances are that small incident may ruin his or her day. To the majority of people, at least in my country, it is considered a sign of good luck and that good fortune is just around the corner.

There are countless ways of interpreting the things that happen to us, what we do, what others do or what happens to them.

Conflicts and negotiations are also included in this general rule or, rather, they are perhaps the most favorable contexts for different opinions and interpretations to arise given any situation.

The Key Is in the Process

♦ Attention and perception are selective. Our personal biocomputer selects and records just some of infinite data sets any situation may offer. The others are either not perceived due to the physiological limitation of our senses or because they have been consciously or unconsciously ruled out. Each individual's paradigms (assumptions, beliefs, and metaprograms) make them very attentive and receptive to those facts or data that fit in with them, while becoming less perceptive or totally blind to those facts or data that do not match.

> *"It is the theory which determines what can be observed."*
>
> Einstein

♦ We remember selectively. Out of all perceived data, we remember those that better adjust to our own theories and preferences.

♦ We interpret selected data. In spite of perceiving the same data, two people from different cultures and differing life experiences may draw distinct logical thoughts about the data.

♦ From particular interpretations conclusions are drawn, ratings and classifications made, beliefs and theories are created, large generalizations are made about things, facts, people and life, all of which serve as filters to perception hence closing the constant feedback circle.

Generalizing/drawing
conclusions

Creating   Creating and reinforcing
interpretations   beliefs/assumptions

Filtering
and selecting data

Figure 10-1   Perception and representation of reality

Even emotions are the result of this way of perceiving, representing and processing reality. Representations of the world and interpretations of what takes place and exists therein are what make people happy or unhappy, winners or losers, all of which makes them feel good or bad vis-à-vis any situation.

> *"Men are disturbed not by things that happen, but by their opinion of things that happen."*
>
> *Epictetus*

If by some mechanism the way of perceiving a fact or processing and interpreting information is changed then conclusions will immediately change. Consequently, the resulting emotions, conduct and behaviors will also change.

In every individual's personal story there surely are one or more facts that for some reason when they occurred were considered a misfortune or greatly detrimental; while over time — and seen from a different perspective, a different standpoint— you discover that it was not so bad, it actually was good or perhaps it was the best thing that could have happened. The change in timeframe, new data ignored in the initial situation, the development of subsequent events, though not changing the facts at all, they *do* change the opinion, emotions, way of thinking and the meaning of such experience.

«One afternoon, while Nasrudin and friends were gathered at a tea room, a monk walked in and said:

"My master taught me to spread the word that mankind will never be fulfilled until the man who has not been wronged is as indignant about a wrong as the man who actually has been wronged."

The assembly was momentarily impressed.

Then Nasrudin spoke and said: "My master taught me that nobody at all should become indignant about anything until he is sure that what he thinks *is* in fact a wrong --not a blessing in disguise! »

A blessing in disguise

Reality, Meanings and Points of View

"In this treacherous world nothing is true or false, beauty is in the eye of the beholder."

Popular saying

There is the reality of things, of facts and events (the territory) inaccessible to humans as a whole, and a suprareality which is the sense or meaning given to things, facts and events; that is, how they are interpreted and the conclusions drawn about them.

In order to manage themselves in society in a more or less orderly fashion, human beings use conventions about things and facts.

Those who belong to the same social group have a series of shared meanings or at least compatible ones called "the real."

Of all possible meanings of a fact or thing, human beings decide on one and operate as a group accepting that particular meaning whether consciously or unconsciously, explicitly or implicitly.

These agreements on meaning, on how to perceive or interpret things enable creating an order or arrangement so as to live in a community.

'To arrange' means to classify, to grasp things from one point of view among multiple possible ones.

Otherwise, everything would be extremely chaotic, variable and unpredictable. For example, traveling would be chaotic if every driver made their own decision to go whichever way they pleased.

All those who share a point of view (a way of arranging facts) accept certain conventionalism about something; they share similar mental maps about various aspects which makes them more prone to understanding. The opposite often causes disagreement and conflict.

Currency, the flag or the measurement system used by a nation all belong to this category of conventionalism.

Words in any language are also conventions. A word is a map or representation of reality, a series of sounds that have a shared meaning that is accepted by a group. Nevertheless, even individuals belonging to the same group and who speak the same language may have difficulties with the meaning of many words.

«The philosophers, logicians and doctors of law were summoned to Court to interrogate Nasrudin. This was a serious case, because Mulla Nasrudin had admitted going from village to village saying:

The so-called wise men are ignorant, irresolute and confused."

He was charged with undermining the security of the State. "You may speak first," said the King.

"Have paper and pens brought," requested the Mulla.

Papers and pens were brought.

"Give them to each of the seven wise men." The pens were distributed.

"Have them separately write an answer to this question: What is bread?"

This was done.

The answers were handed to the King who read them out.

The first said: "It is food."

The second: "It is flour and water."

The third: "A gift of God."

The fourth: "Baked dough."

The fifth: "A nutritious substance."

The sixth: "Nobody really knows."

The seventh: "Changeable, according to how you mean 'bread'."

— "When they decide what bread is," said Nasrudin, "it will be possible for them to decide other things, for example, whether I am right or wrong. Can you entrust matters of assessment and judgment to people like this? Is it not strange that they cannot agree on the nature of something they eat every day, yet are unanimous that I am a heretic?" »

Nasrudin and the Wise Men

If there exist several versions to define 'bread', many more exist to define vague terms such as comfort, happiness, progress, productivity, justice, respect and trust, whose meanings may be unfathomable as are the points of view from which to interpret them or the people using them.

Between Chaos and Inflexibility

While, on the one hand, arrangements make understanding as well as the comprehension of phenomena included in those arrangements easier, at the same time they are able to restrict creative thinking to the extent of becoming immobilized, stiff or blind to other possible interpretations.

Some of Hippocrates' concepts on many diseases, in spite of being erroneous, lasted over long periods only because, knowing who they came from, nobody dared question them.

The Swiss, restrained by their own beliefs, assumptions and conventionalism about how watches should work, were unable to see the value in the idea born among them which, shortly after, resulted in losing their power over the world market, to this day: the quartz watch.

On the other hand, perceiving differently, giving distinct meanings, interpreting things in different ways and concluding otherwise on facts constitutes a threat to the pre-established order and creates insecurity, and, taken to extremes, results in chaos and anarchy. Simultaneously, when done it is a source of opportunities, of new and creative ways of living, thinking and resolving problems and conflicts.

A conventional story tells the case of two shoe salesmen who were sent to Africa to see whether there was a market for their product. Upon arrival, seeing that all the people went barefoot, one of the salesmen sent a telegram reporting: "I'll be back immediately. No one wears shoes." The second salesman also reported back: "Send the entire production. No one wears shoes yet."

Reality and Conflict

Conflicts between human beings are conflicts of meanings.

When two or more people, organizations or countries come into conflict they think they own the truth and believe they are discussing about reality. They think there is only one reality, generally theirs, and they show it using expressions that begin with a paradox "I objectively think…"

The source of many conflicts and disputes lies in the fact that people have forgotten the source of realities; they forget that what is called reality is only an agreement.

Saadi of Shiraz in his *Bostan* stated an important truth when he told this very short tale: "A man met another, who was handsome, intelligent and elegant. He asked him who he was. The other said: "I am the Devil."

"But you cannot be," said the first man, "for the devil is *truly* evil and ugly."

"My friend," said Satan, "you have *truly* been listening to my detractors."

Points of view

The cause of conflict are not facts, unchangeable in and of themselves, rather the different, and occasionally complete opposite ways in which parties perceive, interpret, conclude and arrange facts.

Very different beliefs and values are created if you were born in a guerrilla setting, in the middle of the jungle, having played with guns since childhood and living for 30 years observing events from that angle, than someone who was born in the city, a few miles away from the revolutionary camp.

Yet it is inconceivable to both that the other could *truly* think the exact opposite about something they saw and heard at the same moment. The same fight within a nation with internal conflicts will be perceived, processed and interpreted differently by the guerrilla and the armed forces, so much so as if conflicting parties belonged to two different countries.

Given the same maximum punishment by the sound of a soccer referee's whistle there will ensue different reactions from fans of each team; and certainly opinions will differ between the drivers of two vehicles that have just crashed.

During disputes and conflicts, whether international, commercial or family-related, nobody stops to think that the other side may be perceiving data differently, interpreting information in a different way, making distinct assumptions, and therefore, drawing different conclusions.

All too often, one or both conflicting parties assume that the other has ill intentions, is crazy, whimsical and stubborn or is lying, and both think they are being accurate in their own description of what happened.

The Snake Bites Its Own Tail

When one party believes the other is stubborn, crazy, is acting in bad faith or lying, often that party once again selectively perceives data that supports such theory and interprets each behavior as a demonstration that he or she is right and thus, under such circumstances, the other party cannot be trusted.

Consequently, he or she is distrustful and brings about reactions and behavior on the other side that end up confirming his or her assumptions, like a self-fulfilling prophecy. A cause-effect mechanism hence takes place which is often endless and may provoke escalation of unpredictable consequences, even in situations where differences are initially minor or trivial.

Examples are arms races where countries from different parts of the world get involved for different reasons. Interpreting a fact as a possible threat to a nation's sovereignty encourages its authorities to arm the country claiming to keep and ensure peace. When the others become aware of this action, they feel forced to reinforce their security by purchasing new and more sophisticated weapons, which in turn is interpreted by the other side as a sign confirming that arming themselves was the right decision, and the best move is to buy further weapons.

It is quite common that parties involved in these conflicts are not able to solve this escalation from within the system, i.e. from the same level where conflicts originated. They are almost always locked up in the "same old, same old" game, following the principle "if it doesn't work, use a hammer; if it still doesn't work use a bigger hammer."

The suggested solutions are generally directed towards problems poorly raised since it is not the other side's stubbornness, evilness or falsehood which gave rise to the problem, rather the way in which the brain works, as well as mental processes and different frames of reference each one creates for him or herself.

When nations, companies or people are locked up in these dynamics, they need a new and different point of view, a metaposition, a distinct frame of reference to achieve it; they need reframing.

 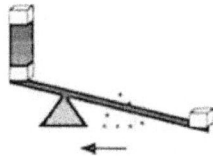

Reframing or Changing the Frame of Reference

Changing your frame of reference or reframing is a term described by the group based in Palo Alto (Watzlawick, Weakland, Fisch, 1974) and refers to the ability or art of changing the way in which facts are perceived or interpreted in a given situation; so that, without changing the data on what happened, it changes the interpretation, the sense or meaning given, and hence its consequences.

According to Watzlawick, "To reframe means to change the conceptual and/or emotional setting or viewpoint in relation to which a situation is experienced and to place it in another frame which fits the facts of the same concrete situation equally well or even better and thereby changes its entire meaning."

Thus, reframing is one of the most compelling tools to change your own or others' opinions on a specific fact or situation, and an invaluable ally for negotiations and in life.

Mechanism of Action

Let us imagine that the brain has a large electronic file of all the things that occur to a person where each fact is classified in folders or files based on meaning.

Given a situation, the senses which are located on the customer service counter of the file receive and deliver data sets to the microprocessor. The processor takes care of interpreting the data and decides what folder of meaning to file it under.

To classify is to place data or data sets into a mental file, a folder of meaning, and then arrange it in a certain way. Once a fact or an object has been filed by the biocomputer within a folder of meaning, it is quite hard to also be included in some other folder or in several simultaneously.

When classifying, possibilities are then limited and other points of view, other meanings of what happened and other possible filing options are lost. From the moment something is interpreted as bad luck and is classified in the corresponding folder, the same individual can no longer consider it as belonging to the good luck or neutral facts category or folder.

On the other hand, the biocomputer is equipped with work simplifying devices and before opening a new file or folder, it will first look to see whether it can include new data received in some previously opened folder or its subdivisions.

Previously opened folders, especially the largest, condition senses when searching. Of all available information, they will cause senses to perceive and consider the one that matches its content, and will induce the processor to interpret it in order to file it there.

The process, following Watzlawick, has different phases:

1. A fact occurs.

2. This fact is framed, that is, classified and included within a category or file of meaning (punctuation) according to an earlier learned process «x».

3. Placing a fact or situation in a certain order, in a frame of reference, makes it very hard to imagine as belonging to another order. A frame does exactly that, it underscores those aspects that are included within the frame, keeping other things outside, whether changing and minimizing their relevance or making them barely visible.

The purpose of reframing is to make one or several people consider a fact, unchangeable as such, as part of another or other types or categories of meaning (file or order), without changing what happened, but leading to conclusions with different consequences and better results for all. For example,

In the bird droppings vignette, the person who was chosen by the bird will certainly feel much better interpreting the fact as a sign of "good luck" and an omen of something pleasant instead of spoiling his or her day; though nothing will change the fact of having bird droppings on his or her shoulder.

Reframing offers a new frame, a different meaning to what happened; it displaces the close-up figure to highlight what was in the background and unnoticed till then in terms of the situation.

The interesting thing about this tool and its special power is that after you have perceived an ignored aspect of a fact, or accepted as feasible a new interpretation thereof and included it in a new file of meaning, you cannot easily go back in your perception, or experience the same previous emotions.

There is a popular ambiguous picture that illustrates the face of two women, an old lady and a young one. After someone who has only seen the picture of the young woman and is willing to strongly argue about what can or cannot be seen in the illustration discovers the existence of the old woman, it is hard to go back to the situation of ignoring the second image, or get involved in the same emotions and uphold a heated discussion as he or she did at first.

The Art of Living

The phrase "reframing, the art of living" was created considering that there is no human activity where this tool may not be applied, and perhaps life itself or human relations cannot be conceived without it.

The list of examples below is just a small sample taken from various fields. The idea is to help you perceive the numerous situations where human beings fall victim to a particular framing, or where such framing is applied, or where you are subjected to more or less successful or more or less elaborate reframing instances.

♦ A negotiation which took place in 1984 between an American and a European company created a tremendous conflict and subsequent lengthy and burdensome lawsuit. The cause: different cultural framing or frames of reference.

The starting point of the discussion was merchandise delivery date by the European company. The delivery date that appeared in the contract was 1/2/84. On January 3rd the American company phoned the other company to ask why they still had not received their shipment. The

European company answered that they did not send the merchandise because they still had one month to go since delivery date was on February 1st.

♦ Professor Fisher tells a story of an invitation he received to lecture together with other celebrities. When the time came for arranging his fees, the person in charge of contracts said to him that payment for the conference was $3,000. As a good negotiator and looking for legitimacy criteria for the offer, Roger asked: "Is that the maximum fee you will be paying the other lecturers?" The response was: "No, there is a speaker who will be receiving $3,500." Fisher asked again: "Is there a special reason why that speaker is being paid $3,500 while I am paid $3,000? Is the speaker perhaps Henry Kissinger who is collecting funds for some charity work?" "No," answered the other negotiator, "but $3,000 is what we're offering you, take it or leave it." "Very well," replied Professor Fisher, "in that case, I won't be lecturing."

A short time later, the contractor phoned him again to say he would pay him $3,500. To his surprise, Roger answered: "All right, I accept to lecture but under the following condition: if during this year you pay another speaker over $3,500 you must agree to pay me the difference." His interlocutor was astounded and stated that such safety clause was abusive and an excess. Roger then replied, reframing: "From my point of view, the safety clause is to your benefit. Truly so, from now on, throughout this year you will have a very powerful argument to defend yourself against anyone who asks for more money to lecture."

A short while back I witnessed the following conversation at a watch store:

Buyer: "I'm not sure, this watch seems fragile and a bit old."

Salesperson: "The truth is, this is our store's classic model; also, it looks very fine on your wrist."

Some time ago I received as a gift a book entitled *The Healing Power of Illness*, which clearly suggests the direction many medical practitioners are taking to reframe symptoms of a disease itself as our body's attempt to communicate something. Instead of cursing the symptoms of stress, this reframing suggests thinking about systems being like sensors that indicate through the pathology that something bad is happening that needs attention and care.

This view reframes illness as a communication with our own selves where symptoms operate on our side and not against us.

As a result of one of the members of a political party leaving the group before internal elections, a party leader stated: "This doesn't mean there are splits in the party, rather that in our internal elections we offer diversity." However, one of the leaders of another party, vis-à-vis a very similar situation said: "Too many candidates weaken the party."

During the speech for presidential nominations, a candidate of the incumbent party (Red Party) said: "You may have seen Reds losing, but never defeated." Along those lines, an army general upon retreating said: "We are advancing to the rear."

One of the most memorable phrases of former President of the United States, John F. Kennedy, was his brilliant reframing: "Ask not what your country can do for you; ask what you can do for your country."

What public prosecutor Kenneth Starr called "adultery", Bill Clinton named an "improper relationship."

All jokes have some reframing that is the essence of the punchline. While the story or narrative leads to a direction and introduces the frame of reference, the unexpected ending changes the perspective, reframing and disclosing what had not even been suspected so far: The Lone Ranger, when seeing hundreds of Indians approach from all directions said to Tonto: "Tonto, I believe we are surrounded by Indians," to which Tonto replies: "What do you mean WE...? Paleface."

♦ For my last birthday I got a birthday card from my children; on the cover there was the smiley face of Garfield the cat and read: "Years don't seem to have passed you by." And when I opened the card, besides my children's signatures it read: "They ran you over."

Advertising is full of reframing instances. Beer-drinking is synonymous with friendship; using a certain brand of powder soap or disposable diaper means being a good mother; and sometimes absurdly relating smoking to sports and healthy living.

♦ Upon careful observation you will find that names of several new business disciplines are really reframing notions. When the term 'downsizing' started to create negative connotations in people's mind, other terms were coined, 'rightsizing' and later 'reengineering', all of which are but reframing of some old-fashioned terms such as 'restructuring' and 'reorganization'.

♦ There is no discovery, creative act or striking solution to a problem that does not include reframing, a change in the frame of reference or an approach form an entirely different point of view.

♦ Lastly, during an important negotiation, one of the negotiators, advised by Professor Fisher, said to the other (simultaneously moving his chair and sitting on the same side of the table as the other party): "We are not confronted; we have a problem in common."

Types of Reframing

There are two basic types of reframing: context and content reframing.

Context reframing

In theory, no behavior or act is good or bad, useful or useless, in any given situation in time or place. Behavior that is considered useless or counterproductive could have or may eventually be useful at some point, time or place different from the current one.

The key to context reframing is the change in time and place where a certain behavior or fact takes place.

For context reframing you need to ask yourself: In what context could this fact or specific behavior have a different value, whether positive or negative? When and where could a thing, behavior, situation or event change its usefulness or rating?

♦ If somebody says: "I'm terrible. I keep forgetting things."

Context reframing seeks a circumstance or context where 'forgetting' has a useful or different meaning from being 'terrible': forgetting about problems and misfortunes is the secret to a happy life.

♦ When negotiating a life insurance policy, agents must create in their prospective clients' mind a frame of reference, a different context from the current one that justifies the investment; otherwise, they would be unable to close the sale.

♦ Garbage in cities used to be a problem until it occurred to someone that in a different context and under certain circumstances it could be used as fertilizer.

♦ "In life, there's no such thing as failure, only feedback," is a phrase that reframes an unpleasant, inappropriate, unexpected or inconvenient event that is taking place into a useful tool as a learning experience for future situations.

♦ Rumor has it that in preparation for Teddy Roosevelt's presidential campaign, his team made the mistake of using a picture of the candidate taken by a particular photo studio and reproduced it into posters for street advertising without proper authorization. When someone noticed this fact everybody thought about the huge cost it would imply to throw away the posters or negotiate with the photographer. Yet the concern was short-lived because it occurred to an advisor to hide that context and create a different one: he called the photo studio and asked:

"How much are you willing to pay to have one of the photos you took of Roosevelt used in the presidential campaign ad?" They answered that although that was not their working policy, given the special nature of the case they would be willing to pay $500.

Content Reframing

No behavior, fact or object means anything by itself, though in fact any meaning could be assigned to it. That is the essence of content reframing. The context remains the same but content meaning changes.

For content reframing you must ask yourself: What unnoticed aspects can provide a different meaning to a fact?

What else can an object, a word, a situation, event or behavior mean? How else could something be defined? How might others see or what might they say about this…? What is the meaning of what happened?

♦ "We are second best that's why we try harder," is a wonderful reframe where being second best, something apparently disqualifying or debasing, means being better for their clients, and becomes the cornerstone of a company's marketing plan.

♦ A young employee at IBM went to see the owner at his office after having made a mistake that cost the company several million dollars, and said: "You probably want me to resign", to which Watson replied: "Are you crazy? This company has just invested several millions in your education."

Reframing in Negotiations

Perhaps more than in any other human activity, negotiations and conflict resolution are favorable settings to use this persuasion tool.

The goal of this segment is to go beyond a list of negotiation examples where reframing has been used as previously presented to explain the concept.

Various common and difficult negotiation situations amenable to reframing will be described and suggestions made regarding the way, mechanism or tools to do so.

Although this list does not cover the full range of possible difficulties one faces during negotiations, at the core they all need to do something different, innovative, contradictory, and sometimes unexpected; something reframing can only contribute to.

Diagnosis: The negotiation is stuck on positions. A position is a way to express what someone wants or needs but there is only one way of satisfying it. For example, "I want 4 million in cash."

Suggestion: There are several ways to reframe this situation.

♦ To discover the interest behind the position.

This is perhaps the most well-known or classic expression of reframing in negotiations. To inquire through questions what the other side really wants or needs, why the party is asking what he or she is asking for, what for, what is he or she going to achieve or attain with it, opens up other possible options to satisfy what is desired.

For example: What will the other side do with the money? What does he or she need if for? Is time an important factor for you in this case?

♦ To interpret the position as an option and directly open the game to other possibilities.

For example: One possibility is for us to agree on that amount and in that way; and allow me to explore other possibilities…

♦ To try to discover the legitimacy criteria underpinning the position, to later talk about the other criteria that support other possibilities.

For example: "Could you explain how you arrived at this figure? What elements did you consider?"

Diagnosis: Somebody threatens to use his or her alternative. Often one or both parties to a negotiation employ threats in order to leave the negotiation and turn to their alternative; that is, what they can do to satisfy their interests away from the negotiation table, whether that possibility is true or false.

For example: "In fact, we don't have to go on with this; I can hire another company to do it."

Suggestion: Reframe changing the game to interests. If somebody threatens to turn to his or her own alternative, you can assume it is because the latter could better satisfy his or her interests than what is being offered at the negotiation table. Hence it is feasible to confirm the reality of that possibility and, in turn, better understand the interests of that side.

For example: "It is true, you could hire another company. Now, let me understand how hiring another company would better serve your interests than hiring us. Tell me more about your interests. What company would that be?"

Diagnosis: Someone raises an objection. Any moment and almost any proposal in a negotiation can be the cause for an objection. All too often it annoys the recipient and, consequently, leads to endless debates that do not result in a solution.

For example: "It could be OK, but I distrust you'll be able to deliver on time."

Suggestion: Reframe changing the statement into a question, disclosing the underlying interest behind each objection and perhaps generating an option with more added value, that is, which results in better and increased satisfaction of parties' interests.

For example: "Do you need a guarantee? Would you be interested in us delivering before that date for a slightly extra cost?"

Diagnosis: Somebody uses dirty tactics to manipulate. Sometimes negotiators seek to reap advantage by using tactics, from the simplest and least creative like making us sit on an uncomfortable chair, lower than others, with the sun glare on our face, going through the good cop/bad cop routine; up to the most subtle forms, making us feel guilty, afraid or indebted.

Suggestion: Instead of reacting, you must diagnose the tactic and reframe.

♦ Expose the tactic with a curious tone: "Is it possible that you may be playing the good cop/bad cop routine here?"

♦ Negotiate on the process, on the way in which you will be negotiating from here on.

Diagnosis: Someone gets angry. Emotions are commonplace during difficult negotiations and anger is one of the most complicated emotions to deal with as it invites escalation to more anger or moves to obedience.

Suggestion: Instead of getting angry or becoming obedient you can reframe and pace the emotion to later lead. We recommend the reader to review the chapter on the Loser Strategy.

Diagnosis: Somebody wants to start bargaining. When reaching the numbers part in a negotiation, almost always one of the parties presses for a discount and haggles over the price in some percentage.

For example: "We are willing to close the deal right now. If we get a 10% discount we will sign now."

Suggestion: Reframe looking for legitimacy criteria. Instead of getting angry or trying to lower the price which is indicative that you are accepting the invitation to play the haggling game, do something unexpected to the other side: through inquiry look for legitimacy criteria and fair reasons that support the request.

For example: "I would like to understand: Why 10%? Why not 20%?"

For example: "The truth is I need your help. Let's suppose I make the discount, how could I explain it to my manager so I don't get fired?"

Diagnosis: Someone does not understand what is happening to others, does not know what they feel or what is wrong with them and does not understand why they are saying the things they say.

Suggestion: Instead of insisting on proposals and arguments that have been futile, you must reframe to understand the other's point of view through the "empty chair" exercise.

Ask someone you trust to cooperate. You place three chairs, A, B and C to form a triangle.

The collaborator must be seated on chair C, or third position.

Sit down on chair A, or first person, and from there, after a brief introduction of the context and situation, say your point of view speaking in first person singular.

When you are done, switch to chair B, or second position, and tell the collaborator what the point of view of the other side is, acting as the other person would and speaking in first person singular. Say for example: "I'm insecure," instead of saying "I think he or she is insecure."

When you are done, ask the collaborator — now that the collaborator knows both points of view — to sit on chair A and play that role; to act as you. And you will represent the other side.

If you follow this process conscientiously, "putting yourself in the other person's shoes", you will probably discover amazing things.

Playing and getting involved in this role provides new information: not only will you perceive how the other side thinks, but also how he or she feels regarding the situation, which will open new perspectives on the problem. Finally, you can ask the collaborator for two new outlooks:

a. From your perspective, what did you think and how did you feel playing your role in the negotiation?

b. From C's standpoint. In that case, you must ask him or her to once again sit on chair C and from there reenact the situation and give feedback on it, especially on the dynamics of interpersonal relations.

Diagnosis: Someone says "no" to a proposal. If somebody answers "no" to a proposal or does something unexpected during a negotiation and you cannot understand why, one tends to think:

♦ The person is acting in bad faith or irrationally.

♦ The person needs to exercise more pressure, looking for arguments to say the same thing or say it louder.

Generally one does not think that any behavior, no matter how absurd, has a positive meaning to a person. The unreasonable behavior of one of the negotiators is the other side's idea, and not the true irrational behavior of the person displaying it. Thus, one tends to skip exploring the situation from the other side's viewpoint and no thought is given in terms of why that person is answering "no".

Suggestion: Reframe the situation thinking that the other side is really persuadable, like any other human being, and if he or she is not doing something it must be for a reason. By devoting time to thinking how the other side sees or considers the situation and if you understand the reason for that person's denial, you will be under better conditions to change the proposal and create another one to satisfy your own interests and enable a positive answer from the other side. In doing so, the following steps are suggested:

- Think what question the other side thinks is being asked and to which he or she is answering "no". The key here is to get as close as possible to the question he or she perceives and not the question you think is being asked or the question you would like to hear.

- After posing the question, draw two columns, one under the label "If I say *yes*", and the other under the label "If I say *no.*"

- Under each column write down what the other side believes the consequences are if the answer is *yes* and which if the answer is *no* to the question being asked.

- Write down a plus (+) sign by the consequences the other side considers as positive and a minus (-) sign by those he or she believes are negative. Given that the answer is *no*, you can confirm that there will be more negative consequences of saying *yes* and positive ones of saying *no*, and it will be clear that if such balance is not altered, the other side will continue saying *no*.

- Considering the information on the resulting consequences, the challenge then is to create a new proposal, invent new options whose content satisfies your own interests but also considering those of the other side, so that saying *yes* has more positive consequences than saying *no* and vice versa.

- Look for legitimacy criteria and objective standards alien to your will or desires that will enable the other side both to feel it is more convenient to say 'yes' to the new proposal and what must be done, what is correct and fair.

- Decide the best communication strategy for the new proposal. When, where and under what circumstances; how and with what means, etc., the proposal would have the best chances of acceptance.

- Search for the best way to tell the other side that time is running against them, that the offer will not get better, rather on the contrary, there are reasons that will lead to reducing its likelihood.

♦ Help build a silver bridge. Think about who would criticize you if your answer were *yes* and what would be the criticism. Create ideas on how to explain your decision if you were in the other side's shoes.

If you were the other side and fail to find appropriate answers to any of the steps, I believe you would continue answering *no*.

Diagnosis: Negotiators argue on conclusions. When two or more people argue at the level of great conclusions, it is futile as it is very hard to persuade under those circumstances. A generalization by one of the parties is followed by a similar or greater one by the other side, in a useless, never-ending game. It becomes a verbal escalation that entrenches participants and occasionally ends up damaging the working relationship. In such cases, the reason for stagnation is:

♦ One or both parties rush into a diagnosis which is perhaps mistaken or subjective in terms of the problem and its causes.

♦ One or both parties jump directly to a positional solution proposal.

When this occurs, the course of the negotiation may become complicated given that any of the two situations or both combined limit possibilities and creative thinking, often limiting the negotiation; especially if what is being said is posed in absolute terms leading to ineffective confrontation escalation for real problem-solving.

For example: (Department X) "We deserve the majority of the bonus because we made greater efforts than you did."

(Department Y) "You're crazy. The truth is that you made the contact with the client and we did the hard work."

(X) "Hard? No! Your work is mechanical. Our work is creative."

(Y) "Yes, but we fix the mistakes you make, that's why we deserve 80% and you 20%. That's the equation we propose; it's fair and what's reasonable in this case."

Suggestion: Do not react by arguing the conclusion, reframe:

♦ Understand and expand the other side's frame of reference. Look for data and interpretations the other side made of them to reach their conclusions.

Ask the other side, interestingly seeking their point of view, their perception of reality, subsequent reasoning, and listen actively in order to understand though not share.

For example: "What are you considering when you say you are making more efforts? What are you referring to? What makes you conclude that?"

Similarly do so with your own case. When expressing a conclusion, explain to the other side what data from reality is perceived and what you are taking into account, as well as interpretations that lead to drawing certain conclusions. Seeking for a point of agreement at the data level is infinitely easier than agreeing on conclusions.

♦ Use the linguistic metamodel tools of the chapter "Did you get it? No!" to challenge verbal transgressions disclosed, to understand what the other side really wants to say when saying what it says.

For example: "Let me understand, what 'hard work' means in this case specifically? What mistakes are you specifically referring to and how are you specifically correcting them?"

♦ Use the four quadrant tool.

Given a problem situation, diagnosing in which quadrant it is convenient to place the conversation is a tool to start reframing. If someone is drawing conclusions, more often than not the conversation can be placed in quadrants II or IV relative to problem diagnosis or solution. The idea is to reframe by taking the conversation to another quadrant.

♦ When the conclusion refers to a categorical diagnosis (quadrant II) do not fall into the initial temptation to try to destroy it. Rather move to the signs and symptoms quadrant (quadrant I), aiming to find out what signs and symptoms the other side has taken into account to reach such conclusion, as well as diagnose which have remained outside their own frame of reference enabling them to draw different conclusions.

For example: "What data are you considering to make such statements?

Have you considered...? How are you evaluating...?

♦ When the conclusion refers to a specific or position-based solution to a problem (quadrant IV), do not assume it is the only possible solution and discuss it as such. Instead, move to quadrant III for possible solutions and change the proposal from a single one to a possible one.

For example: "That equation is a possibility. Another possibility is to name an impartial person, one we both trust in terms of judgment and balance, so as to establish objective criteria and mediate in this case.

We could also move to quadrant II to understand and eventually question the diagnosis the solution seeks to tackle, or even go back to quadrant I in search of data considered for such diagnosis." Then, you can go over quadrants clockwise to frame and underscore new data (quadrant I); other possible diagnoses or causes (quadrant II) and other possible solutions (quadrant III) that contribute more creativity and added value than the previous proposal for both parties.

For example: "Another possibility is: instead of splitting the money we could use all or part of it to improve the bank's daycare program which all our children will benefit from and probably, too, our future relations. We could even set up a committee so that, calmly and considering all available data and information, it may create rules to establish how to divide future bonuses any department may qualify for."

Diagnosis: Somebody articulates a "nightmare" phrase. A "nightmare" phrase in this sense means a phrase that encloses the combination of a situation diagnosis and an inconvenient solution in negotiation, both enclosed in a cause-effect relationship or a complex equivalence; that is, one thing is equal to another or a current fact has been caused by a previous one. For the causal relationship to be true and the rationale legitimate for acceptance, certain conditions must take place. If, among others, the cause invoked is insufficient to produce the effect or outcome; if there might be another cause; if at any time different effects were demonstrated and if causality cannot be proven, it is thus possible to think and generate new options.

For example: A consulting job is being quoted and the client notes: "You charge a lot. I can't spend that much."

Suggestion: Reframe by using one or several of the following linguistic tools:

♦ Question definitions and redefine: Replace one of the key statement terms or phrase by another with a similar meaning yet with different implications.

For example: "This isn't an expense, it is really an investment."

♦ Point out the possible negative consequences: Direct the other side's attention to the negative consequences of the person's statement.

For example: "Have you thought of the resulting expenses if the conflict goes unresolved?"

♦ Focus on the intention. Focus your attention on the positive (or negative) purpose or intention of the cause-and-effect relationship defined in the statement.

For example: "The idea is certainly to seek the best cost-benefit relationship."

♦ Use a counter example: Find exceptions, one or more examples that do not match the relationship defined in the statement.

For example: "Buy cheap pay twice. Allow me to tell you what happened to me once..."

♦ 'Fractionate' into smaller units, trim down: Go from a specific
element to a more specific one. Break down into smaller elements so as
to enable a change in the cause-and-effect relationship defined in the
statement.

For example: "What part of our proposal would you be willing to
contract?"

♦ Generalize, enlarge: Go from a specific term to the general category it
belongs to.   Show the inclusion of an element into a broader
classification or order.

For example: "Any good consulting work is always an important
investment."

Find a more important objective: Help the other side discover a more
significant objective. Defy the relevance of the statement and change to another
objective or topic of greater potential value.

For example: "When you must confront the hardships you are faced
with, the point is not to pay less but rather to hire the most appropriate
consulting firm and solve the problem."

Use an analogy: Find a simple (or metaphorical) analogy to the defined
relationship, but having different implications.

For example: "Many people thought like you when they hired the new
coach for the French soccer national team, but they became world champions."

Go one-up in the criteria hierarchy: Reassess the statement based on
criteria that may be more important than the one used in the statement. Show
that the proposal seeks to meet that higher value in its order.

For example: "I am sure you agree that it is more important to solve this
conflict fast and in an environmentally friendly way than saving a few dollars."

Change the size of the time frame: Reevaluate statement implications in a
larger (or smaller) time frame.

For example: "I understand it may seem expensive today, but over time,
when you measure the benefits, this will result negligible."

Assign the consequence a different cause: Reassess the statement from a
different perspective, establishing a new cause-effect relationship on the same
statement.

For example: "It is possible you may think you can't afford it because you
have no faith in yourselves."

Apply the other side's logic: Use the same relationship the other side uses, switching the cause with the effect and vice versa.

For example: "The truth is that your idea of being unable to spend so much may end up costing you more money."

♦ Use another reference: Reevaluate the statement from another model's standpoint, from a different perspective.

For example: "It might seem expensive but people with consulting experience will tell you it's a fair deal."

♦ Defy reality: Look for the perceptions used by the other side to build that reality.

For example: "How do you know it is expensive? Compared to what specifically?"

Final Recommendation

Diagnosis: You wish to apply reframing in or outside a negotiation.

Suggestion: Do not use "Yes, but." Elegance and coarseness do not get along well.

Reframing is the art of what is possible, a way of opening up your mind to new and better possibilities for both parties to a negotiation.

If used with ingenuity and talent results will be positive for both parties.

If used negatively to pursue and corner the other side, then a chapter should be written on the art of obtaining poor results.

> *"Some see the glass half empty, others see it half full. I believe the glass is too big."*
>
> George Carlin

In Summary

Nobody can completely get rid of all stressful or difficult life situations; yet, it is possible to generate resources to deal with them.

Throughout the various chapters in this book I have tried to put forward some ideas, concepts and tools taken from the fields of psychology and combined them with a negotiation methodology to help resolve more efficiently and elegantly conflicting situations one must inevitably face throughout one's lifetime.

The topics presented are by no means the only ones to be considered within the goal set out, but those included here can help to:

♦ Generate a relationship of trust, credibility, empathy and good atmosphere in negotiations. Without these conditions it is difficult to attain good results.

♦ Know how to usefully sort out people you will be negotiating with and their negotiation styles by using some data, so that you may not only predict some of their answers and behaviors but also, through flexibility, increase your persuasion capacity, adjusting the communication and strategy to the ways in which the others see the world, and to their language.

♦ Be equipped with an important resource to dismantle anger situations and, rather than escalating aggressiveness, be able to defuse the mechanism and lead the situation rationally to more efficient resolution ways.

♦ Avoid misunderstandings during the negotiation process and beyond, when parties need to live up to their agreement.

♦ Try to change from a reactive to a proactive attitude in order to first diagnose what is happening and then answer, looking to combine what we like with what is convenient and legitimate to do.

♦ Get out of old negotiation patterns, especially when they have not achieved and are not achieving good results, and change them for a more flexible and assertive style based on an effective method and a win-win philosophy.

♦ Think and discover the risk taking capacity as well as how not to go from one extreme to the other: Move from the absolute paralyzing conservative mode to a fearless attitude where no consequence is estimated.

♦ Know how to detect and defend yourself from manipulations, especially those like guilt and bribery which are hard to perceive under cover and hidden, and, in turn, be equipped with a method to enable achieving what you want without needing to manipulate others.

♦ Recognize whether what you are practicing in negotiation is really a ritual where both moves and the ending are predictable: a psychological game played through different roles (persecutor, victim or rescuer) aimed at pursuing a pseudo benefit or an activity; that is, a series of transactions led by an informed adult who works with a method.

♦ Get involved in the fantastic field of all things being relative, in the world of means of perceiving, interpreting and concluding about what happens, the source of our misfortune, happiness or good fortune. Find ways to change, not facts which are unchangeable, but meanings, hence creating more options for influencing, leading, resolving differences and achieving a better quality of life.

Finally, the purpose of this book is to put forward different ideas, new options, more possibilities, more vulnerability, trusting that each person will know how to discover, take and adapt the concepts and tools considered useful. In contrast to a computer, no virus will erase the resources each of you already has, so the only thing that might happen is for the reader to expand his or her repertoire. That is the final goal.

Words of wisdom

«A delegation once went up to Nasrudin's house to ask him to give a talk to the town people.

"What would you like me to talk about?" asked Nasrudin.

"Well, that's not important," said the delegates. "We want you to tell us a few words of wisdom."

"Very well," replied Nasrudin, "please gather the people on Friday afternoon at the square and I shall speak to them."

On Friday a crowd gathered at the square and when Nasrudin appeared, there ensued an awe-inspiring silence.

"I have some words of wisdom to say to you," started off Nasrudin, and at that moment silence was such you could not hear a pin drop.

"Would you like to know how to earn money without working, have knowledge without studying, and skills to do things without practicing?"

People started looking at each other, at first surprised, then enthused and finally started shouting louder and louder: "Yes, Yes. Of course we want to know!"

"Well then," replied Nasrudin, "If I ever get to know how it is done, I'll come to the square and tell you about it." »

CHAPTER 9

DON'T KILL BUTTERFLIES!

A Strategic Guideline to Resolve Conflicts in Situations
With Apparently Little Negotiating Power or…
"Cunning Is More Than Strength"

The Butterfly Effect

> "The flutter of a butterfly's wings in one end of the world may set
> off a tornado in the other end."

> "Sit the parties to a negotiation or parties in conflict side by side or
> in an angle at the corner of a table and place a pad or a flipchart in
> front of them facing the problem."

> Prof. Roger Fisher

When Roger Fisher used to repeat this advice in his Harvard classes, I always thought it was an interesting recommendation, especially since it is so different from what you generally see in these types of situations where parties to any negotiation (even more so if it is a conflict) typically sit opposite each other at the table.

"We are confronted," is the silent yet powerful nonverbal conveyance of these scenes that are sometimes reinforced using flags, shields or signs that identify and represent factions in conflict and mark their respective territories.

"We have a problem with each other" say those papers on the table intercepting both parties where each has written "his or her" version of the subject, his or her own point of view, and judging by the way they are seated you could assume it is "contrary" to the other side's.

Whoever is in charge of organizing the room's arrangement or the negotiation table itself hardly knows, can or dares do anything to change this situation, this very inconvenient way of starting off the negotiation.

Many times it is even those absurd protocols which dictate where, next to whom, or facing whom, etc., such and such a government or company representative or official must be seated.

When dealing with delegations or negotiation teams, even if there are no rules or territory markers like those mentioned earlier, it is interesting to observe how those belonging to a faction or group, following a natural almost ancestral instinct, once in the room they get together, cluster and look to sit far apart from the other side, with whom oftentimes they do not even have differences; they simply do not know each other.

To the contrary, the scene which Fisher suggests implicitly generates *communication*, a totally different message. Without need to delve into many or sophisticated interpretations, this psychographic negotiator arrangement conveys the following message to the eyes of any observer: *"The problem is not between you and me, rather you and I have a problem in common that we need to resolve."*

The Huge Power of Subtlety

Is it possible that something so small and so subtle like changing the place where negotiators to a conflict sit could achieve such a dramatic or really significant effect?

The truth is it can.

To measure the possible outcome of a small change in the negotiation process based on its "apparent" size can be a tremendous mistake.

Life itself is full of examples where a minimal change in the process may dramatically affect results whether it is preparing a recipe, the human gene or communication and interrelation in a complex negotiation.

In their book *Seven Life Lessons of Chaos*, Briggs & Peat describe how Edward Lorenz, a meteorologist and one of the founders of the theory, was testing a simple model for predicting the weather using only three elements: wind speed, barometric pressure and temperature, yet used in three paired equations so that the results of one fed into the following.

It seems that Lorenz had made a long calculation and needed to check the results. Since back then there were no speedy computers like the ones currently available, Lorenz decided to take a shortcut in calculation and considered three instead of six decimals. He assumed that this tiny change in calculation could introduce an approximate 0.1% error in the results from a mathematical standpoint and, of course, he expected a similar degree of error in his weather forecasts.

He was tremendously surprised to realize how little this new prediction had to do with the first one performed using 6 decimals. He quickly understood it was the repetitive feedback mechanism between equations (a circular cause and effect mechanism) that accounted for such distinct forecast results.

This phenomenon known by mathematicians as a *"nonlinear system"* (circular) and known in psychology as *type II change or change of change* or *metachange* (P. Watzlavic, R Fish et al) is what motivated Lorenz to become one of the pioneers of the well-known *theory of chaos*.

While in linear systems cause and effect relationships are generally predictable, in "chaotic, nonlinear systems" the slightest particle, a small error or subtle change, *the flutter of a butterfly's wings*, may, in certain circumstances, explode unpredictably hence changing the entire system and leading to absolutely unexpected consequences, as were the results of Lorenz' calculations.

This way of looking at things is not for many of us the customary way of thinking about problems, resolving conflicts or seeing the world in which we live.

On the contrary, not only is our thinking commonly regarded in absolute linear terms but oftentimes it goes hand in hand with a very short term view, and almost blindness to the long term effects some of our actions have.

A great majority of the tremendous environmental issues we are faced with today are based on the combinations of linear thinking and a short term view of the results or effects of some of our actions.

We do not believe how something we do today, because we think it is small, may have surprising or unpredictable consequences in a more or less distant future, or we do not even find a relationship between both phenomena.

Conversely, we do not appreciate that something "small" done or applied at the right time and place could resolve very complex problems, a long standing conflict or change the world.

There is a reason for this way of thinking.

A) The truth is many problems we are faced with daily are resolved by thinking or reasoning linearly, by a mechanism whereby cause and effect are quickly and clearly perceived as being related.

If someone at home feels cold, you raise the heat; if that person is still cold, you raise the heat some more and, generally, in such system and following a linear logic, the situation is at some point resolved. However, in human systems, contrary to heating systems (mechanical), things do not always work that way, for better or for worse. For example, all those who read this article must have experienced some sleepless night. A linear logic such as "cold/ heat / cold / more heat," would suggest, as the sleeplessness solution, something along these lines: *If you are sleepless "try" to sleep, if you still cannot fall asleep, "try harder."* I am sure all readers are also aware of the results of such tactic.

Another example: How do you think a person who is depressed feels when a friend or relative, following a linear logic says: "Hey, come on, brighten up, change that look on your face, it's not so bad, cheer up, and don't get depressed." And, if this doesn't work, you tap them on the back and more energetically try to cheer them up.

That person will not only continue to be depressed but most certainly will worsen, since in addition to being depressed his friend or relative is implicitly saying that he or she does not know how to measure problems at hand, that his or her reaction to the situation is exaggerated and his or her attitude is not sensible.

Like in other examples, following this linear logic we sometimes fail to solve our conflicts or differences and even worsen them. The rationale "*if at first you don't succeed, get a bigger hammer*" does not categorically apply to many cases.

This is the logic and mechanism behind many war escalations (symmetrical escalation) where the linear thinking system may last obsessively for generations leading to total hopelessness of those involved or related in terms of the chances of peaceful problem solving.

Some of these problems or conflicts "seem" to resist all efforts made and *"resistance is persistence."*

Most certainly in these circumstances, all those involved are trapped in the reasoning, applying once and again the same solution to a problem poorly raised, involved in what chaos scientists have called a *limited cycle or closed system.*

Almost crystallized like a fly in a piece of quartz, they perpetuate a behavior robotically, reinforcing a useless or unsuccessful pattern, worsening the situation with the *same old, same old* behavior.

B) Sometimes distance or time separating the cause from the effect is the reason why we fail to perceive their relationship and *circularity.* Disasters occurring in companies resulting from plans created by short-term, social climbing managers are often perceived when the latter, paradoxically, are promoted to a superior position, often overseas, or when he or she no longer belongs to the company having retired as a hero. Many of the environmental disasters human beings are now creating will have evident manifestations years ahead, and some of the problems we are experiencing today originated in unthought-of actions out of ignorance, or criminal actions carried out decades back.

C) Other times, it is the apparently negligible size of the cause which makes us lose sight of its relationship to something that is taking place now. Those of us who are allergic (currently a majority) and those who luckily are not —yet probably know someone who is—, know exactly what I am talking about. As a doctor I have served and seen people die from an anaphylactic (allergic) shock after eating a single shellfish or by the sting of a bee. What happened? A chaotic, circular (nonlinear) cause and effect system dictated such a tremendous outcome faced with an initial tiny stimulus.

"God and the Devil Are in the Detail"

In these open systems, everything is interconnected and subject to amplification, splitting, change and repetitive positive or negative feedback circuits so that suddenly what we considered unlikely, unpredictable or impossible occurs and explodes in front of our faces.

Thus in life, generally, (as well as in those conflicts we are involved in) we cannot perceive or understand how some of our own actions are determining factors of sometimes undesirable or other times favorable results to our own interests.

We think that in order to solve sizeable problems we must "always" apply also sizeable or highly complex solutions (the greater the nail, the larger the hammer) which certainly is "sometimes" required but often times is not.

We occasionally consider such great goals that they become utopian or impracticable (we wish for peace or happiness in the world), or we create a deadly trap imposing on ourselves or onto others to present "the best option" or "the best idea" to resolve a problem.

In conflicts and negotiations, stimulated by our own logic in pursuit of linear solutions and all too often to seek *the* solution, we not only create and increase problems but also distrust and rule out solutions due to their shape, size, oddness, the moment in time or even who suggested them. We fail to understand or refuse to admit that something apparently negligible, or so tiny or subtle to go unnoticed, can actually produce such surprising effects. Yet, fortunately or unfortunately it is thus: *"God and the devil are in the detail."*

We skeptically state: How could the location of the negotiators at the table have a bearing on this terrible problem that lasted dozens of years?

All too often, with increasing contempt, we rule out our power to do something, sometimes that of others' and occasionally of all, by skeptically saying: *"nobody can fix this"* hence starting off or reinforcing the closed system.

However: *"No man is an island."* John Donne.

"We are part of the whole. Each specific element has a bearing on the direction of all other things in the system. The power of the butterfly enables the impossible." *"Through chaos an individual or a small group of individuals may profoundly and subtly influence the entire world."*

J. Briggs and F. D. Peat

One of the keys to overcoming that feeling of hopelessness, contempt or impotence that floods many conflicts and problems that seem irresoluble, is precisely to think that even from a seemingly week or powerless position a smart and sometimes apparently negligible action may have unexpected effects and may influence the entire system.

Some years back I was called to facilitate a meeting between a group of laying hen breeders or egg producers.

The situation was as follows: For many years they had been involved in a price war that led them into a "limited cycle" or closed system. The only mechanism everyone had found to improve their individual situation was to lower the prices their supposed competitors had established in the market.

By doing more of the same they had reached a point where they were not only gaining little revenue but losing money. They had generated a true "symmetrical downward escalation" where the war was not waged with bombs, mortars and missiles; it was "a price war."

At the time I came into contact with the situation prices were so low that each producer lost in average 1 dollar per each 30-dozen egg case. The estimated loss adding all producers was a monthly $600,000 ($7,200,000 a year.)

The mechanism was really wicked since, as imaginable, the decrease in price did not go hand in hand with an increase in consumption; nobody will eat four fried eggs instead of two because egg prices are really low. The only ones in the market who benefitted from this situation were their intermediary clients, including large supermarket chains.

Attempts had of course been made to agree on a price increase, but the result of each attempt and each agreement made was betrayal by some producer who thought linearly that lowering prices would increase sales and hence take advantage, short-term, of the competition without weighing the long term consequences of his action on the system.

Sometimes I think that the circuit did not even start by a true betrayal. They were so untrusting with each other that many did not pay heed to their clients when these tried, using the "divide and conquer" routine, to tell them that so and so (another producer) had offered them a better price. Without confirming the truth of what clients were saying, producers reacted by lowering their prices and starting, for real, the true chain of betrayals and self-fulfilling prophecies.

We began our morning work with the group of producers, doing an awareness exercise on issues such as credibility, trust, managing assumptions, determination on how we define who "we" are and who the "others" are, as well as some other subjects I thought convenient to deal with considering the situation at hand.

When the exercise was over I went on to illustrate what I believe was what changed the repetitive dynamics of that closed circuit and created a turning point in the development of events.

I estimated how much $600,000 meant in terms of eggs per day, per hour, per minute and per second.

The resulting amount used to represent the loss incurred by the group on a monthly basis was 6.5 eggs per second. I had someone prepare 10 clear nylon bags each containing 6 eggs, as I was unable to include half an egg (at least not natural ones) and kept the bags hidden until noon.

When I decided it was a timely moment, I asked one of the producers attending the meeting to please do me a favor and count 10 seconds, one at a time, out loud and using his watch.

Each time he counted a number I would crash one of the 6-egg bags on the floor until I completed the tenth and last bag.

As you may imagine, on the one hand it was a mess because some bags were unable to resist the impact and burst spilling all content. On the other hand, producers were also unable to resist the impact.

As each bag fell to the floor, one by one, the faces of all those present transformed. Some slight smiles at the beginning gave way to expressions of surprise and ended up with real serious countenances when little by little they began to realize what that metaphor enclosed.

The quiet scene that ensued was moving. Silent and glued to their chairs they listened to me in a way I had seldom been heard before.

Yet my words explaining to them it was what they were doing in real life, destroying at an extraordinary speed and through a wicked system what they produced with so much work and efforts, at times felt redundant.

Though it might seem almost incredible, after lunch they signed an agreement on pricing; something they had stopped trying for quite a long time.

However, in everybody's mind there remained the question whether they would live up to the agreement.

Consequently they requested a new meeting with me aimed at facilitating future negotiations, and especially to examine what they could do to ensure agreement continuity.

In that meeting, after talking about their goals and some ideas on the process I proposed to them, they asked about my fees, as was expected. I told them I would charge them whatever consulting hours the process would require at the current CMIIG fees and, in addition, if we achieved the minimum goal which was to stop losing, they would have to pay me 10% of actual losses during one month, that is, $60,000 dollars.

In summary, they came out of the meeting willing to think about it, but I did not get that contract, neither did we work again on that subject.

However, the latest news I heard from them was that they lived up to their agreement and that they had increased their prices to $8 per case, all of which clearly surpassed the minimum initial goal to stop losing.

What brought about the change? Despite not having really facilitated any discussion session or formal negotiation, what happened? What made things change unexpectedly and favorably for the group?

One could argue that many factors came to bear in this outcome, and so it was. Yet, the missing condition, what effectively triggered change were two seemingly "minute" events (which in some other version of this story might not even be recorded) and the "butterfly effect" in action.

The first, "the omelet" scene, showing the result of their price war which changed the abstract perception of an amount of money ($600,000) to something tangible, measurable and evidently painful for what it meant to a producer: destroying 6.5 eggs per second.

The second significant event was realizing that in order to help them do what they could perfectly well be doing alone, they would have to pay me $60,000, and, knowing their nature, it would go against the thrifty and conservative philosophy of this group of farmers.

An open system and the butterfly effect took care of the rest.

♦ **An International Case**

The former president of Ecuador, Dr. Jamil Mahuad and Prof. Roger Fisher met at Harvard when Mahuad attended one of the famous negotiation courses.

When Mahuad was the mayor of the city of Quito, he met several times with Fisher in that city during one of Fisher's trips to Ecuador.

As soon as Mahuad was elected President, he called Fisher and said: "Roger, we must put an end to this damned boundary dispute. It's very hard for the world community to provide us with the support we so need while we're purchasing planes to fight against Peru. I want to end with this conflict."

Till then, Mahuad had never met with Fujimori, they did not know each other personally.

Roger traveled to Ecuador a short time before Mahuad traveled to Paraguay where he was to meet with Fujimori.

Once again proving his renowned ingenuity, Prof. Fisher made two seemingly small recommendations to former President Mahuad which created *the* difference in this well-known and till then unresolved international conflict.

The first question Fisher posed was, *"What is the purpose of this meeting?"* Mahuad answered that his initial goal was not to fix the entire problem, "I want to meet him first," he stated.

*"Well then", said Roger, "if you ask too many questions, he might feel he is being interrogated. I believe it would be easier to get him to know you first since that is something under your control. You could let him know that **they** have a seemingly better case than you with the arbitration that took place in 1945, and since he has served as President for more years while you have just come into office a few days ago, you need his advice and help; given that you will not be able to accept his position unreservedly before the Ecuadorian Congress."*

It would certainly be hard to find a better or more fit example than *"the loser's strategy"* in action. In a relationship that had till then featured a symmetrical escalation where an arrogant or belligerent attitude of one of the parties was followed by yet another more arrogant or belligerent one, Fisher suggested a totally different approach. He suggested: instead of showing your teeth, expose your neck; instead of attempting to strike a blow, show them your other cheek.

I can imagine the effect, surprise and ulterior consequences this subtle and unexpected suggestion had on the Peruvian president who surely envisaged an Ecuadorian president similar to previous ones who had not even tried to know him and negotiate with him personally.

"If I were in your shoes I would try to get a picture of both sitting side by side, not standing, not looking at each other, not looking at the photographer, not smiling, not shaking hands. You should sit together, holding and looking at a paper pad or perhaps at a map. Each one of you holding a pen pointing at the paper you are both working on. That is the photo I would recommend."

This was the second recommendation Prof. Fisher gave his former student.

I agree with Prof. Fisher that this picture made an impact on the public when it was published in the first edition (No. 334) of *El Universal* newspaper of Ecuador. The impact must have been greater on the people at the border and upon the military men who guarded it, as it most certainly had on the two presidents when they saw each other differently, *working together.*

"To me," says Fisher, *"building a relationship is on the one hand to show that you are not enemies or adversaries. You are trying to solve the problem together; both are concerned about the same issue."* After this meeting, Fujimori called Mahuad once a week to talk, when apparently the former had never spoken to any previous president.

It is not easy to change a game featuring an adversarial dynamic to one of collaborative problem-solving but I think this photo helped in that regard. The public image was important: these people are not fighting each other, they are working together. It was a move that changed the game.

Two subtle but ingenious moves, an open system and the butterfly effect did the rest in solving a conflict that lasted over 45 years.

Power: Dominance or Influence?

Power is a very hard term to define when we seek to do so through the great variety of expressions in real life.

One of the most common ways of expression, or perhaps the one we are mostly aware of or able to perceive, is power as control or dominance over things, nature or other people.

If we have such kind of power we feel the illusion of security; if we don't, the illusion is one of handicap or impotence.

Yet life is full of examples that suggest that open systems, chaotic systems, that is, natural systems (including social ones) cannot always be controlled or predicted through that type of power.

There are ways out of complex problems that might take place at the start of a seemingly small action which, subjected to sometimes visible, others inadvert feedback circuits, create the paradoxical power of subtlety, the power of the butterfly.

As a new example, taking the context of Prof. Fisher's case and beyond any political connotation or value judgment, let us consider the long standing impossibility of former President Fujimori's opponents to change the Government of Peru.

Traditional methods —including some violent acts like those when Fujimori took office after being reelected for an additional five years— achieved nothing to change the political reality in Peru. Nothing seemed possible to reverse the situation, not even the power and pressure exercised by international organizations like the O.A.S.

Yet a minute video camera (a butterfly) placed at the right time and place were enough to achieve what had been impossible till then for all opposing parties and powerful international organizations put together.

The videotaping of some "unholy" meetings of Montesinos, one of the closest collaborators of the then President Fujimori, destroyed his government; put Montesinos in jail and Fujimori was exiled to Japan.

When to Think About the Butterfly Effect? Limited Cycles

Theory of chaos experts define *limited cycles* as those natural systems that somehow seem to be closed because a great majority of their energy is used up when reproducing over and over again the same unsuccessful behavior patterns.

This phenomenon is universal and independent of time; it affects all systems regardless of their scale or size. We can observe it in the heart of a family, a company, a country or even in the behavior of an individual who transits life repeating over and over again (with seeming variations) the same failed behavior.

These systems seem to resist all efforts to change them.

The problem lies in several aspects:

♦ Disqualification

"They can because they think they can," used to say Virgil.

Those who believe they can and those who believe they cannot are both right. Those who believe they **can** are *sometimes* right and sometimes not; those who believe they **cannot**, are *always* right.

It only takes those participating in a difficult conflict or negotiation to disbelieve in their capacity to resolve it for the conflict to endure.

This mechanism known as disqualification has different degrees. Sometimes you can discredit your own capacity to solve something but may think that some other person might eventually do it. Other times, you can discredit the chances of a specific third party resolving the problem. Lastly, you might eventually be able to discredit the chances of a problem being solved by anyone.

It is hopelessness, giving in when faced with the seeming persistence or size of the problem, the reason for the impossibility in resolving it.

A closed circuit lives on to the extent that everyone has given up their creativity based on wanting to keep obsolete system rules that seem impossible to break or change. All stiff, closed, crystallized systems whether conflicting or not, in order to persist depend on us believing that we cannot do anything to change them.

Those self-fulfilling prophecies of system members are the ones that keep the situation alive.

In order to keep the situation going you only need all members of a group to keep within the comfort zone, not defying what is pre-established; no one should ever ask: What would happen if...? And when someone does, he or she is harshly critiqued once and again, or told that it is absurd or irrational.

♦   Dependence

A variation of disqualification is the sense of dependence, instead of the feeling of interdependence.

If our thinking and reasoning is linear, if under a frame of power interpreted as control and dependence we perceive ourselves as a piece of the classic corporate organization chart, that is, as part of a pyramid-like structure where perhaps we do not sit in a place of seeming authority, it is very likely that we might not even perceive the slightest chance of contributing or effecting change, and we might confuse authority with power.

Conversely, if we considered ourselves as part of an interdependent whole, as part of a network where each individual element flows and is influenced by the rest through infinite and complex interrelations, we would realize, to a greater or lesser extent, that we are all constantly influencing and being influenced.

We all have power in interdependence.

Who controls the Internet? Is there any authority present like the one we are used to seeing governing countries or companies? On the contrary, there are thousands of users, suppliers and service customers who interdependently manage, create, change and bring life to the network.

Thousands or perhaps millions of people buying and selling stock from different parts of the world will soon render the majority of stock exchange moves unpredictable and will cause power disappearance of the so-called "experts"; except where people continue believing in self-fulfilling prophecies.

Under these circumstances, the contribution of an individual or a small group might change the world, and history is full of examples where, like Christ or Gandhi, they earmark a before and after period.

♦   Iatrogenic causes

Iatrogenic is the technical term used in medicine to describe those diseases or problems caused by treatments physicians indicate or maneuvers we perform. Occasionally, the problem caused by a therapeutic or diagnostic procedure is so great that we can definitely apply the well-known and popular saying: "you cut off your nose to spite your face."

Yet, sometimes in these crystallized systems, the remedy is not worse than the disease, rather "the remedy *is* the disease." The original causes of the problem remain lost in the history of time, often distorted and occasionally even forgotten by current players.

They are the solutions themselves with which they attempt to fix problems that keep them alive and perpetuate them.

Those weapons bought by a nation for "defensive" purposes supposedly justify the purchase of more weapons by the neighboring country who perceives such "defensive" effort as a "threat" thus getting involved in a symmetrical escalation with an unpredictable ending.

Those measures to control or do away with the production, sale and use of "illegal" drugs are the ones that raise market prices, generate the temptation towards the forbidden and enthuse increasingly more producers and sellers to enter into and grow the business.

♦ More of the same

"If something fails, try something else."

If you wish to be more indulgent you might say that if something fails, try again, more emphatically or with more enthusiasm, but if even so it leads nowhere, think and act differently.

"*Madness,* "said Einstein, "*is doing the same thing and expecting different results.*"

Perseverance is undoubtedly a great human virtue, yet persisting in the mistake results in catastrophic consequences.

When a larger hammer does not work, think whether the problem is not really the nail.

Distrust what is obvious; if after diligently trying for several minutes to fall asleep and fail, try getting up, read a good book, play some good music, listen to what your unconscious has to say; write something, plan your next vacation or whatever comes to mind; it will certainly be more advantageous and, you never know, perhaps you get bored and get sleepy.

♦ The grandiose solution

Long-lasting or very complex situations and problems make us believe that only spectacular, overall, grandiose solutions may fix them. This frequently paralyzes us because we think that what we are able to do, compared to what supposedly is required, lacks any sense. However, this type of grandiose thinking is what often falls into the domain of utopian reasoning and in turn limits the creativity of subtle solutions. Coupled with our fear of making mistakes, of saying or doing a likely foolish thing, such thinking paralyzes us.

Yet the solution to many problems and conflicts often comes about through a period of great uncertainty and chaos, but with freedom and allowance to think even in the wildest, most minute or absurd solutions, as the cases referred to earlier.

As if we were carving into a huge raw diamond, these situations typically require a slow, detailed and careful analysis. Then a small, sometimes slight tapping of the blade in the right place is enough to obtain one or several pieces of unfathomable value (or else, if the situation was inappropriately analyzed, some disposable stones.)

All the factory's machinery had been stopped for several days and none of the mechanics "hit the spot" in operating the intricate maze of pipes, valves, cables, manifolds, lights and connections.

Determined to put an end to the costly losses the factory stoppage was producing, they called in an outside expert of international fame and very well-known for his extravagances and high prices.

The famous mechanic went around the factory attentively looking at different sectors, carrying only a small toolbox out of which he took a hammer at a given point.

He then slightly tapped a valve and, magically, the whole chain of iron pieces and gears started operating seamlessly.

Everybody's happiness at the factory only declined when they received the bill for $10,000.

The plant manager quickly phoned the mechanic and asked how he could charge $10,000 for a slight tapping of the hammer.

*The mechanic then replied: "**The truth is, for that slight tapping of the hammer I'm only charging $1 dollar; the remaining $9,999 are for knowing exactly where to tap.**"*

When I was speaking with Dr. Richard Fisch at the Mental Research Institute in Palo Alto (California) and asking his advice on an extremely complex conflict, he told me the following story, by way of recommendation, which, in my mental files, finds no comparison to better sum up the core concept of this chapter.

"Have you seen lumberjacks throw tree logs to the river so the water drives them downstream to the sawmill or port?" *"Yes,"* I answered.

"Did you notice how sometimes the logs get stuck against some rock and a tremendous jam ensues with thousands of logs that seem to form a huge island?" - *"Yes,"* I stated once again while the picture appeared clear in my mind.

"Well, "said Fisch, *"in order to free that huge jam you don't need to move those thousands of logs; just one or two will do."*

CHAPTER 12

Credibility and Trust

**Reduce the Complexity
of Your Negotiations and the World**

12

The Basic Feeling of Our Times: Psychological Fear

We live in a world that has become extremely complex for the great majority of its dwellers and that complexity is perceived as threatening.

Many people feel more vulnerable today than ever before. They do not know or cannot manage with reasonable skill their daily coexistence with uncertainty. This ends up reflecting in life which, at the most, is unsatisfactory. Such dissatisfaction is sometimes explicitly expressed and others through a huge amount of psychosomatic pathologies, chronic stress and its short, medium and long term consequences on health and living together. Though the phenomenon is more complex and has many variations or conditioning factors, the unlikelihood of reasonably predicting the future is one of the factors that complicate our existence. Psychological fear is the fear experienced in the absence of a real threat or a specific and pressing situation of danger, and to many people it is the basic emotion of their lives.

That fear of what life or the future has in store for us, or fear of what I think could happen but is unknown to me, sometimes hides behind depressive conditions (open expression of a dwindling self-esteem); or on the contrary through anger, fury or aggression to oneself or to others (hidden expression of a weakened self-esteem.)

If everything changes so rapidly, if the rules of the game are not abided by or are in constant change, if the only persistent thing is change and if I can expect almost anything from people, organizations or institutions I relate to, chances are I will not handle myself adequately, or my body will end up responding with anguish and anxiety.

The increase in sales of antidepressants and anxiety pills worldwide confirms this hypothesis.

On the one hand, such a world calls for getting prepared and training ourselves to better manage uncertainty. This is a long personal road that starts off by accepting the reality of how things are regardless of whether they are not to our liking or what we believe they should be.

On the other hand, it requires some balance, leveling out and reducing the causes of uncertainty and the feeling of vulnerability, where possible.

Striking a Balance

Restoring the lost balance of a chaotic world and reducing uncertainty require the application of *complexity reducers*.

Our entire life is full of them though we might not perceive them. For example, the traffic lights at each corner in our cities have among other functions the one of reducing complexity and curtailing the number of possible responses of a more or less large set of conductors. If left to our own free will we would turn each crossroad into a five bullet "Russian roulette". The simple agreement to circulate on the right hand side (except in England and some other countries) is another great traffic complexity reducer; straightforward, yet very effective. It could be equally effective if drivers stuck to their lane instead of zigzagging. All these mechanisms are in place to make behavior predictable; not abiding by these complexity reducers results in driving with a constant feeling of uncertainty and risk.

It is believed that Carl F. Gauss, a famous German mathematician, had a brilliant mind since childhood. One day at age 7 his primary school teacher, in an effort to gain time and get onto other tasks, posed her students the following problem: what is the sum of all consecutive numbers from one to a hundred?

The teacher expected to keep the students pretty busy adding $1 + 2 = 3 + 3 = 6 + 4 = 10$, and so on.

Much to her surprise, a few minutes after giving the assignment Gauss raised his hand and answered: the result of the sum is 5050.

The teacher was astounded not only because the result was correct but also for his expedited completion of the task. She asked him how he arrived at that result and the bright boy showed her the blackboard where he had worked out the solution and said: "I added $1 + 100$ which equals 101, then $2 + 99$ which equals 101 and then $3 + 98$ which also equals 101, so I said to myself, how many pairs of 101s are there in this set of numbers? Fifty. Hence fifty times 101 equals 5050."

Reducing the complexity of the world often requires some geniuses as Gauss; other times only actions closer in range to those of us regular mortals are required, like the traffic lights example.

Among the overall complexity reducers there is none, in my opinion, that is able to do it more efficiently, radically reducing the complexity of the lives of people, companies, countries and negotiating processes as…

Trust: The Great Simplifier

The term *confidence*[1] comes from the Latin *con* (full, all) *fides* (faith, trust.); *confidere* (have full trust.)

The dictionary of the Royal Spanish Academy defines it in the following entries:

Firm hope and belief or trust in somebody or something.

Reliance on and faith in oneself, confidence in own vigor and strength.

Vain opinion or proud of oneself.

Familiarity, relationship based on familiarity.

Though originally it might have been an interpersonal concept, it has currently extended to many other fields. It is clear that we speak of trust in systems (organizations or countries), in political parties, ideas, technology, science, broadcasting, a brand or an individual's competence (separate from the person), international standards (ISO 9000 or similar) or even fiction elements like money.

In fact, the notion exists or is present in almost everything we do though its involvement might be outside our conscious perception. It would suffice to grasp the notion if we were to imagine waking up one morning and as a result of happenings during our sleep we no longer trusted anybody or anything.

Can you imagine how life would be like if we were to distrust the alarm clock to wake us up at the exact hour? Or if we doubt whether the milk we drink is pasteurized or that drinking water isn't really fit for drinking, or if we thought it might be poisoned? Or perhaps the bus that goes to the airport suddenly has a different destination and might take a route other than the regular route? Impossible, right? I dare not picture the conversation you would have with your partner over breakfast that morning!

---

[1] TN: Spanish term *confianza*. Translated according to the entries in the Dictionary of Spanish Language of the Royal Spanish Academy or DRAE.

The notion of trust floods or affects (by its presence or lack of it) almost all types of relationships. With the exception of relationships governed by absolute power and control such as a prisoner with the warden, or in past times a slave with his or her "owner", all other relationships whether family, social or work-related require trust to survive.

It is the quality that bonds relationships such as physician-patient, or lawyer-client, parents-children, teachers-students, friends, spouses, members of a team, customers-suppliers and bosses and collaborators.

Any relationship that requires mid and long-term thinking must be based on trust and credibility among parties in order to function. And all "complex" negotiations —which represent the great majority of our important life negotiations—, are based on trust.

We negotiated in the past, negotiate today and will continue negotiating in the future whether with individuals or organizations. Experience shows that personal or working relationships not based on trust oftentimes can only be sustained by force; otherwise they tend to disappear or fall apart.

The value, importance and pervasiveness of trust are undoubted and separate from the size of the system we are involved in; what changes is its form.

When we speak of small organizations, groups or communities, what matters is the notion of familiarity, that members know each other personally and they trust in their "word"; formalities and rules may not be well taken, even mentioning them may be tantamount to lack of trust and hinder the negotiation process.

In larger and more complex systems (large organizations, groups, cities, etc.) it is highly unlikely to manage ourselves with familiarity, without rules, laws, decrees, contracts, and lawyers or civil-law notaries in whom we place our trust.

Whatever the size or shape of the system, if trust is endangered the entire system will be in danger.

When speaking of negotiations, we say that trust is at stake when:

• We depend on others to obtain what we need;

• We have no control over the situation;

• There is the likelihood of betrayal and in fact,

• The benefit of betraying is greater than living up to what was promised.

Alternatively, if satisfying my interests or needs is not dependent on the other; or if I have control over the other person's behavior by whatever mechanism; or if the other can in no way betray me; or if doing so is less convenient than what was agreed to, it is clear that whether or not there is trust, the outcome will be the same.

The existence or lack of trust in the great majority of complex negotiations does make a difference.

When there is trust among negotiating parties potential behaviors are reduced and predictability increases.

Trust prunes away all futures; it reduces the potential futures to some that are more likely or more "certain", according to each case. Parties' free will thus remains limited. Out of all the things someone in whom I trust could ultimately do, I think as a minimum, that person will *not* do those things that might hurt or be detrimental to me.

We have all at some point witnessed —and experience also shows us daily—, that when there is trust between parties to a negotiation or to any type of relationship, decision-making is facilitated and becomes more efficient, and the system gains time.

When a system places things in the trust "bucket", it no longer has to think about them, and saves on resources which it would otherwise have used for monitoring or supervision.

Consider the difference between receiving a report from someone you trust or from someone you distrust; or reviewing and controlling a statement from a credit card you trust and one you distrust. Trusting enables the reduction of complexities in interrelations and allows for gaining resources which parties will use to ultimately create new complexities or new developments; it enables the energy to be placed outside, in external problems or opportunities and not using up energy for internal issues.

When there is trust in negotiations the value creation circle enlarges both in time devoted to the elements that compose it as well as in results attained from the exploration. Negotiators spend the majority of their time exposing and inquiring on interests, creating good options for mutual gain that leave nothing on the table, and suggesting legitimacy criteria to solve differences fairly and equitably.

Alternatives rarely come up and thus threats to leave the negotiation table are less frequent.

Commitments on the substance are delayed in the process when anxiety is reduced. This enables an increase in time spent exploring possibilities to first enlarge the size of the pie and develop creativity, separating the process of inventing solutions from the decision-making process. The latter will follow and will be based primarily on legitimacy criteria agreed to by the parties.

When there is trust, communication is more efficient; in fact negotiators do not waste their time in "sizing each other up" as boxers during the first rounds of the match, nor do they take forever to resolve a problem that can be solved in a few hours' time.

When there is trust, the expected negotiator behavior is transformational: "moving towards" and achieving things that motive them, more risk-taking, hence increasing opportunities for future joint gains.

Conversely, when there is *no* trust, the most frequent behaviors are conservative: "avoiding", "moving away from", geared toward reducing risk and tending to dig into their position. Often negotiators are more in pursuit of not losing rather than winning; they become curt when it comes to showing their interests and generating creative options grows scarce or nil. They spend much time sizing each other up, saying vague things in order not to compromise themselves, all of which makes communication inefficient and the working relationship tense. Alternatives are constantly on their mind and consequently the threat of leaving the negotiation table pervasively hovers over them.

This change in behavior appears, noticeable in negotiations where trust is an asset and those where there is no trust, because lack of trust is generally not translated into a "neutral" state from which negotiators work devoid of problems; lack of trust is frequently expressed under the shape of distrust.

Distrusting in turn implies a mental energy which though unconscious for the person experiencing it, is hard to hide from other parties. We all know from our own experience that distrusting not only wears you out, it has that almost relentless tendency to increase, escalate, to self-perpetuate and even to bring about self-fulfilling prophecies: that which is feared or suspected to take place.

The Competitive Differential of the Near Future

For all of the above, generating a relationship based on trust and credibility is not just another factor to consider in the negotiation process, it is one of its cornerstones. Its existence or lack of it affects to a greater or lesser degree the remaining elements that comprise it.

It is not a question of generating trust and credibility because it is nicer when both do occur, or simply because it is good to be a reliable person or company, rather it is a matter of cost-benefit.

In a turbulent, fast-changing, unpredictable, uncertain and scary world, people and organizations will bet on and pay more to those organizations, people, or products and services that are more reliable. Knowing how to build a trusting relationship will in the near future be increasingly more profitable; trust will be more and more on demand and will be the differential factor with the greatest power in increasingly competitive markets.

By the Grace of the Holy Spirit?

When we ask ourselves personally what trust really is, how do we know when we trust in someone or something?   Regardless of the dictionary definition, many of us would say it is *a feeling*.

We would say that trust is something we feel, and some of us might even be able to describe in more or less detail the feeling we experience when it is present, and point to that part of the body where we feel it.

Yet, we all know that trust also relates to *judgment,* an opinion we create based on our experience regarding behaviors displayed by a person or organization, a product or service.

However, if trust also arises as a result of judging or evaluating facts and actions, then it is possible to generate trust based on certain actions and not wait for it to appear by the grace of the Holy Spirit, which may mean it might never appear.

The fact that trust may be created should not pose the slightest doubt if we consider our own self-esteem, i.e. the most basic trust, the trust in ourselves, caused by the way in which our parents, tutors, siblings and teachers, etc. raised us.

It is worth pointing out at this moment that both people and systems show a greater or lesser predisposition to trust externally (which is) proportionate to their inner trust and security (self-esteem).

People and organizations with good self-esteem operate better not because they suffer less setbacks or disappointments than the rest but because they have greater tolerance to them. They are not alien to problems; they are better able to resolve them assertively. Neither are they unmindful of world uncertainty, rather they experience an increase of bearable insecurity. Self-esteem or self-confidence acts as an internal complexity reducer.

Building Credibility and Trust

If our trust results from judgments made based on actions of individuals or organizations we relate to, then our own actions are in turn the means to generate trust in others.

Hence the question is: What things must specifically be done or avoided in order to build trust and credibility?

The following recommendations are not limited to those included in the list so it is not intended to imply there are no other things that can be done or that these are the best. It is mostly an example and a trigger for new and better ideas, and especially to do away with the belief that trust is something magical and that we do not know where it comes from and how we lost it.

Similarity: If trust can be defined as familiarity, familiarity then is related to similarity. "When in Rome do as the Romans" goes the wise saying, and this can be extended to clothing as to words used, to the tone of voice as to body gestures, to the volume of our voice as to the speed of motion or posture. Although it is much more powerful to share values and beliefs, similarity in simple aspects like those mentioned earlier is, occasionally, the secret language of success in negotiations. Sometimes the fact of sharing information on similarities in the personal realm may lead to strong emotional bonding and greater trust between conflicting parties coupled with the resulting benefit for potential problem-solving. Such was the remarkable and contemporary case of two high ranking military officers of two countries at war. During the introduction and warm up exercise at a Harvard Seminar, they both discovered that one of their respective sons suffered from the same illness. Although neither of the two was able to correctly introduce each other as cued because they had forgotten to request other personal data, creating this human connection based on commonalities outside the negotiation was crucial to the meeting's outcome.

Note: To explore this subject further, readers should turn to Chapter 1 of this book: Do Opposites Attract?

Active listening: To listen in order to understand, to ask good questions showing interest and respect, to paraphrase, to make sure you understand what is being told and that you are in turn understood, are all powerful tools at the service of building trust. Active listening in negotiation and in life in general tells the other that "you matter to me" too. If I matter to someone it is reasonable to think that person will not do something to harm me. Active listening helps build trust by increasing the chances of predicting behavior, among other beneficial effects.

Predictability: To reduce the risk of possible answers when faced with a given situation; being predictable. It is a powerful recommendation for building trust though it may be interpreted as contradictory or "all or nothing" thinking types. Your question to this suggestion might be: "What you are saying is that the company should be more unbending (or myself), that I should lose flexibility and latitude in such a changing world? Are you asking me to be unyielding in my negotiations?" The answer to these questions is: Be flexible when it is convenient, for example in your marketing strategies, but be predictable when speaking about your organization's core values. Be firm and share values such as love in the family, or cooperation and teamwork in the company or solidarity in the community. In these subjects, it is good for everyone to know where to find you at all times in order to increase credibility and trust; you should be really predictable. The same holds true when you negotiate. Remain open and flexible to generating creative options; open your mind to new ideas or to accepting legitimacy criteria, but be predictable and firm on the type of process you wish to advance, to principled negotiation abolishing the use of deceitful tactics and pursuing a win-win goal.

Clear and respected rules of the game: In December 2001, in the middle of a severe economic and institutional crisis, a public emergency situation was decreed in Argentina; the Government established a series of sudden economic measures which basically restricted account holders to withdraw cash from their bank accounts thus forcing them into high use of banking services. Money transfers overseas were forbidden and the then 1 ARS= 1USD convertibility scheme was abandoned. Finally, the Government converted all dollar deposits into pesos and established that all certificates of deposit, checking and savings accounts were to be paid through bonds and certificates of deposit with varying maturity.

These measures coupled with a great currency devaluation policy suddenly drove a critical mass of citizens into savings dilution. Uruguay went through a similar crisis in 2002, partly as a result of the regional impact of those measures and partly for local reasons. Therefore, in capitalist societies such as these where for whatever reasons the basic rules of the game are suddenly and forcefully changed, asking people to trust, to invest, to generate business and take risks is like "trying to get blood out of a stone." First they will have to get everyone out of the trenches where they obviously all went the moment they lost trust in the system. Those people that were able to withdrew their money from banks and placed it overseas, or hid it in the most unbelievable places, even digging holes in their backyard. Establishing and complying with clear rules of the game is a key element for organizations as well as for governments. How an organization measures success should be revealed to employees and abided by. Employees should know for what actions he or she could be punished or rewarded as well as the existing promotion (or dismissal) system. Being aware of job descriptions or the performance assessment system in place is crucial when attempting to build trust and credibility. You must ensure that your decisions and those of the organization's leaders are fair and transparent, and you yourselves must follow the established rules. You will notice how trust has a domino effect or rolls like a snowball. The way in which managers negotiate with their people and resolve differences leads the way in which the people negotiate among themselves and resolve their differences. Make rules be known by all and apply them equally to all.

Professionalism or competence: Being competent and professionally managing what you do generates trust and it is easy to understand how decisive that aspect is for some choices, for example, when choosing a surgeon. Though under certain circumstances it might not be easy to be fairly assessed by a third party lacking training or information, it is worth investing in professionalizing what we do if we are interested in building credibility, even the way in which you conduct your negotiation processes. Sales teams, purchase teams, management or entire companies who negotiate "professionally" using a consistent model and tools with their respective measures of success create a great impact in the market based on their clients' trust and credibility. These organizations look to negotiation skills (competencies) as a prerequisite when selecting, rewarding or promoting their staff, and it is pervasive in job descriptions and performance assessments.

Frankness. Honesty: Our internal and public speech must match; what we think and feel must be directly related to what we do and say; in short, practicing what we preach is an amazing trust-building quality. Being honest, not bragging about ourselves or our skills, appropriately showing limitations of our knowledge, when handled masterfully are invaluable allies of trust. For example, in certain academic or company settings that deal with knowledge as their primal tool, being honest and sincere about what we know or not know or about our strengths and weaknesses is of paramount importance. If we say we know it all surely nobody will believe us. It is best to speak out clearly about what we know and don't know before being put in a spot and give way to others who are knowledgeable on the subject. Not lying is a thousand-year-old recommendation by the wise men of humanity and is valid for life in general, including your negotiations.

Honor your commitments. Responsibility: The value of living up to what you have promised, of honoring agreements and commitments barely need an explanation when considering them as potential trust generators. You could be very competent and even sincere when negotiating but if you make commitments that you cannot or are not willing to live by, it all falls apart. Thus our recommendation is to always commit yourself prudently on issues regarding substance, after having thoroughly explored interests, options and legitimacy criteria, and reach an agreement only if what is on the table is better than your best alternative. Even so, we must always make sure that what we have agreed to is realistic, comprehensive and functional; that is, it is able to be complied with, containing all that is necessary and without leaving anything out or unclear, and where it undoubtedly expresses what each party has to do or not do, when and where.

Introducing the long term: Always keep the long term vision in mind; long term consequences of today's actions help parties weigh the value of trust in their negotiations or relations in general, like in a virtuous cycle. Not perceiving these aspects has led humans to endanger our own existence on earth, to embrace an immediacy philosophy and to try to benefit without measuring consequences, an attitude which we have extended to organizations and interpersonal relations including our negotiations.

Faith and trust go hand in hand and we all too often use them as synonymous terms. I have faith in you is synonymous to I trust you. Exercising faith, having a strong belief in life beyond life, looking to and trusting in a transcendental future beyond the limits of our own existence helps many people overcome terrestrial shortcomings with more serenity. Many organizations have built a similar sense about the future; they have found a way to generate trust in the current times by developing a long term vision shared with their people. Looking after long term favorable or unfavorable consequences both in negotiation results and how the process is being carried out will help strengthen the importance of trust as a determining factor for success.

Make trust an important value in your organization: Ensure that reliable behaviors become "the way in which we do things in this organization." In doing so you must find the way to measure and reward those behaviors. When we arrive at this point the typical objection is: The problem is that trust is a very subjective issue. Even so, considering the difficulties implied in measuring something subjective, and beyond the fact that trust shares this quality with many other human things, weighing this factor sends a clear signal to all about its importance. If you wish to build a setting of trust and credibility, do not get tempted by, "slick cunning", though short term results of some of these negotiations may be seemingly good. I assure you they never are in the long run. Do not reward wise guys, dirty tactics or someone else's taking advantage of you in a negotiation, not even smile at the narrative of such an action. Reward those who act with integrity. Include reliability in your performance evaluations; promote this value by making public at any possible occasion good examples that have been rewarded and poor ones that have been punished.

Show trust: Along the same lines of the principle developed in the chapter "The Obscure Principle of Reciprocity", showing trust and good faith in someone helps that person feel the need to be reliable or loyal correspondingly. When appropriate, taking some risk in this aspect may be very beneficial.

You are probably asking yourself the following question:

When Is It Right to Trust?

Another way of expressing this same concern is by taking things to the extreme and asking: Must I always trust everyone?

Our answer is an absolute and downright "no", as absolute and downright as the answer to the question: Must I always distrust everyone?

What is paradoxical when dealing with trust is that it seems one should trust in those cases or circumstances where trust has been earned, and this once again leads to the first question. Unfortunately, I do not have and I do not think you will find a recipe that will enable you to say in which specific negotiations or whom to trust, how much and how far.

Well then, trusting always includes some betting; it is somewhat risky and this is part of its nature and impossible to separate. This is an inborn difficulty of the system and not a problem.

Yet, I have a friend whom when told that a training is costly, he answers, "if training seems expensive to you, then try ignorance." This is much the same, if you think trusting is risky business, then try distrusting, and you do not need much to do so.

The previous suggestions are truisms, I do not have to prove to you that they work; just try doing the opposite of what they suggest and you will see the consequences of entering into the world of distrust.

We will never recommend trusting blindly; we propose instead to be worthy of trust, to be reliable 100% of the times. There is tremendous power in negotiations and in life when you are reliable, and just as I assured at the beginning, people will pay more for those individuals and organizations that are reliable. Being reliable is worth it.

Trust is a current account into which you must make deposits daily and carefully see that you are never in the red because, contrary to bank checking accounts, the majority of the times there is no way of recovering broken trust.

Trusting our model is part of a general and broader strategy we highly recommend in your negotiations and significant relations. *Being unconditionally constructive.*

This means doing what is good for you, for the other side and for the relationship, regardless of the other side acting similarly.

"Friends Unworthy of Trust"

> *You do not need to ask yourself whether you should befriend a person*
> *who is unworthy of trust.*
>
> *A person who is unworthy of trust is nobody's friend.*
>
> Idries Shah (Reflections)

CHAPTER 13

Negotiation:
A Tool at the Service of the Ego

A Recipe for Guaranteed Suffering: "Not Knowing What You Want and Exerting Yourself to Attain It"

Upon completing some of our negotiation workshops I usually ask participants why they took the workshop. Their initial answers are quite varied.

Some attend out of a wish to grow their organizations, others want to resolve a specific problem ahead, others look to improve their transaction outcomes with clients and suppliers, and many wish to enhance their relations in a variety of contexts, even within their families; and so on.

If I am insistent and after each answer I ask "Why do you want what you say you want?" this process invariably leads to the final shared reply which is: to be happy.

All the previous answers are but intermediate answers on the road to the primary objective which is: every human being's pursuit of happiness.

This answer, of course, is the single answer that requires questioning no further "what for?"

There is no further response to the question "why do you wish to be happy?" than the redundant answer: to be happy.

Now, if I were to ask all participants the question "what exactly is happiness?" having agreed that the final goal of what we do in life is searching for happiness, I often get vague answers, cheap rhetoric or no answer at all.

The latter situation is really striking because how can you pursue something throughout your life which you cannot say or define clearly what it is.

Yet it is not less striking to have an unclear or mistaken definition, or believing that attaining happiness is something almost as magical as a fairy tale.

Incredibly enough the majority of people transit their lives absurdly valuing happiness as the most precious asset and do not set aside even a moment to seriously ponder about it or about which roads lead to such goal.

Their suffering is unfathomable just by ignoring what are the essential conditions that may lead them to attaining what they so desperately seek.

What is most tragic is that the majority of participants to our workshops are really experts in problem-solving and in creating plans to achieve goals and objectives.

They know that in order to obtain something they need to prepare intelligently and be very keen on details. However, some people never apply what they know or their skills to their life's problems or their primal objectives.

Even if they lacked the required knowledge and skills, it is important to know that any trade can be learned; and that of being happy can too.

Definitions are the key.

Many definitions are really deceitful since they are roads that lead anywhere but to happiness.

A lot of people unconsciously take as a reference for their own happiness the single thing at their reach: what they watch on TV, or what appears in soap operas or what they read in cheap fashion or design magazines.

Yet other apparently more orthodox definitions may be equally poor when wanting to know what to do to achieve happiness.

The Royal Spanish Academy Dictionary says that (*felicidad*) *happiness is the mood or state of mind that takes pleasure in possessing an object or good.*

This particular definition certainly translates one of the common mistakes the majority of humans make regarding the subject, and it is due to a lack of knowledge by a small group of members of the Royal Spanish Academy of Language (Spanish acronym, RAE).

The Spanish Academy's definition is the definition of the universal ego per se.

The ego (individual and collective) confuses happiness with possessions and positions: Your own house, a brand new car, a new television set, graduating, a job appointment, the first million, marrying Prince Charming...

Nevertheless, we all know by our own experience that not only is it possible to be happy without having to possess anything, on the contrary, possessing (oftentimes in excess) does not guarantee happiness, and, in some cases, renders it impossible.

We also know, in fact, that our wishes have no limit.

If we have a TV set we want two, if we have a 26" one, we want a 32-incher, if it is a regular screen we want the flat screen, or even better, a plasma screen, if we have the latter we wish for a home theater set, and so on.

This weakness enslaves us, and even worse it fills us with fear.

We are fearful because we do not know whether we will be able to attain what we wish, and we are also afraid of losing what we have already attained.

If you are afraid you are not free, and if you are not free you cannot be happy.

Finally, wishing or desiring to possess something permanently places happiness in the future.

The ego believes that what is to happen in the short, medium or long term will bring about happiness and says: *When such a thing happens..., when I'm able to achieve...,when, when, when...*

Unfortunately, when that future (which only exists in our imagination and may never happen) finally arrives, it finds us wishing and desiring new things, so the ghastly mechanism prevents us from enjoying what we have already achieved.

Wise men of all times have said that, contrary to what the dictionary definition recommends, possessions are more of a hindrance than a facilitator of spiritual development and the achievement of happiness.

In fact, those wise men *"have always lived simpler and poorer lives than the poor themselves."*

Their understanding is that happiness means inner peace, poise and quiet.

Being happy means being free from passions and desires.

Being happy means living without fear and fear is the basic emotion of a life that circles around possessions, wishes and aversions.

"Happiness and bliss are produced not by great riches nor vast possessions nor exalted occupations nor positions of power, but rather by calmness of mind, freedom from pain, and a disposition of the soul that sets its limits in accordance with nature."

Epicurus

Therefore there is an inner definition preexisting the pursuit of wishes to become negotiation experts, and it is thus:

Are we going to improve our skills to polish our own ego or to be happier?

By all means it is better for our ego to use interest-based negotiation to achieve what it wants and not, as some political leaders do, decide to use weapons and create a war to attain it.

Negotiating well is of course much better for resolving conflicts than being aggressive, and it is even better than having to manipulate in order to indirectly achieve what we cannot otherwise do directly or assertively.

Now, if the interest to learn a proven model and tools when attending one of our negotiation workshops is aimed at serving an unlimited ambition, the task that awaits the participant will continue to be endless.

It will even be the source of further problems than existing ones if the workshop is used to achieve what the ego loves, that is, to compare yourself to others (I am a better negotiator because I studied at CMI International Group in Cambridge.)

Neither our model nor any other model will allow you to reach something it has not been designed to do, that is, fulfilling an unlimited capacity to desire.

If your ego understands that happiness in life is achieved by possessing things or attaining fame and power, the negotiation skills you subsequently develop will only be a good solution to an ill posed problem.

They will never lead anywhere but to transient contentment and guaranteed mid and long term suffering.

You will become more skilled in suffering further.

Whereas if you have attended our workshop in search of a tool that will help you be happy; understanding that happiness means achieving calmness, living in peace with yourself and your surroundings — including other humans, animals and the rest of the planet—, then our model will prove excellent.

As you see, it is all about an inner definition, perhaps an earlier determination before attending the workshop or purchasing one of our books.

"For a person is unhappy either from fear or from unlimited and vain desires. But restraining these may secure the contentment of reason."

Epicurus

Bibliography

BANDER, Richard and John GRINDER: *La Estructura de la Magia*, Santiago de Chile: Cuatro Vientos Publisher, 1980.

CIALDINI, ROBERT B.: *Influence: The Psychology of Persuasion*, New York: Quill, William Morrow Publishers, 1993.

EPICURUS: *Sobre la felicidad*, Barcelona: Debate Publisher, 2nd ed., 2001.

FAIRHURST, Gail T. and Robert A. SARR: *The Art of Framing*, San Francisco, California: Jossey-Bass Inc. Publishers, 1996.

FISHER, Roger and William URY: *Getting to Yes: Negotiating Agreement Without Giving In*, Boston: Houghton Mifflin Co., 1981.

FISHER, Roger, Elizabeth KOPELMAN and Andrea KUPFER SCHNEIDER: *Beyond Machiavelli: Tools for Coping with Conflict*. Cambridge, MA: Harvard University Press, 1994.

HALEY, Jay: *Las tácticas de poder de Jesucristo y otros ensayos*, Barcelona: Ediciones Paidós Ibérica S. A. Publisher, 1991.

KOUZES, James M. and Barry Z. POSNER: *Credibility: How leaders gain and lose it, why people demand it*, San Francisco, California: Jossey-Bass Inc. Publishers, 1993.

KERTESZ, Roberto: *Análisis transaccional integrado*, Buenos Aires: IPPEM Publisher, 1997.

KERTESZ, Roberto, Clara ATALAYA and Victor R. KERTESZ: *Liderazgo transaccional*, Buenos Aires: IPPEM Publisher, 1992.

LABORDE, Genie Z.: *Fine Tune Your Brain: When everything's going right and what to do when it isn't*, Palo Alto, California: Syntony Publishing, 1988.

LORENZ, Konrad: *Hablaba con las bestias, los peces y los pájaros*, Barcelona: Labor S. A. Publisher, 1991.

LUHMANN, Niklas: *Confianza*, Barcelona: Anthropos Publisher/Universidad Iberoamericana, 1996.

MOINE, Donald J. and John H. HERD: *Modern Persuasion Strategies: The Hidden Advantage in Selling*, Englewood Cliffs, New Jersey: Prentice-Hall, Inc. Publisher, 1984.

O'CONNOR, Joseph and John SEYMOUR: *Introducción a la programación neurolingüística*, Barcelona: Urano Publisher, 1992.

RAIFFA, Howard: *The Art and Science of Negotiation*, Cambridge, MA: Harvard University Press, 1982.

RICARD, Matthieu: *En defensa de la felicidad*, Barcelona: Urano S.A. Publisher, 2005.

RICHARDSON, Jerry: *The Magic of Rapport*, Cupertino, California: Meta Publications, 1987.

RUSSELL, Bertrand: *La conquista de la felicidad*, Buenos Aires: Debolsillo, 1st ed., 2007.

SUN TZU: *El arte de la guerra,* Madrid: Fundamentos Publisher, 1981.

TÁLICE, Rodolfo V.: *Etología práctica,* Montevideo: Ediciones de la Plaza Publisher, 1988.

URY, William, *¡Supere el No!* Colombia: Norma Publisher, 1993.

WATZLAWICK, Paul: *Change: Principles of Problem Formation and Problem Resolution,* New York: W. W. Norton & Co. Inc., 1974.

WATZLAWICK, Paul, Janet BEAVIN BAVELAS and Don D. JACKSON: *Teoría de la comunicación Humana,* Barcelona: Herder Publisher, 1993.